The Housing Crisis

Series Editor: Cara Acred

Volume 253

Independence Educational Publishers

First published by Independence Educational Publishers

The Studio, High Green

Great Shelford

Cambridge CB22 5EG

England

© Independence 2013

British Library Cataloguing in Publication Data

The housing crisis. -- (Issues ; 253)

1. Housing--Great Britain.

I. Series II. Acred, Cara editor of compilation.

363.5'0941-dc23

ISBN-13: 9781861686596

Printed in Great Britain

MWL Print Group Ltd

Contents

Introduction

The **Housing Crisis** is Volume 253 in the **ISSUES** series. The aim of the series is to offer current, diverse information about important issues in our world, from a UK perspective.

ABOUT THE HOUSING CRISIS

For 22- to 29-year-olds across England, the average deposit required to buy a home is a whopping 229% of their net annual salary. Despite schemes introduced by the Government, young people are still finding it extremely difficult to get on the property ladder and increasing numbers are renting rather than buying. The UK also faces a severe shortage of adequate housing, with many social housing tenants living in overcrowded conditions. This book explores the housing crisis in the UK, looking at causes and possible solutions.

OUR SOURCES

Titles in the **ISSUES** series are designed to function as educational resource books, providing a balanced overview of a specific subject.

The information in our books is comprised of facts, articles and opinions from many different sources, including:

⇨ Newspaper reports and opinion pieces

⇨ Website factsheets

⇨ Magazine and journal articles

⇨ Statistics and surveys

⇨ Government reports

⇨ Literature from special interest groups

A NOTE ON CRITICAL EVALUATION

Because the information reprinted here is from a number of different sources, readers should bear in mind the origin of the text and whether the source is likely to have a particular bias when presenting information (or when conducting their research). It is hoped that, as you read about the many aspects of the issues explored in this book, you will critically evaluate the information presented.

It is important that you decide whether you are being presented with facts or opinions. Does the writer give a biased or unbiased report? If an opinion is being expressed, do you agree with the writer? Is there potential bias to the 'facts' or statistics behind an article?

ASSIGNMENTS

In the back of this book, you will find a selection of assignments designed to help you engage with the articles you have been reading and to explore your own opinions. Some tasks will take longer than others and there is a mixture of design, writing and research based activities that you can complete alone or in a group.

FURTHER RESEARCH

At the end of each article we have listed its source and a website that you can visit if you would like to conduct your own research. Please remember to critically evaluate any sources that you consult and consider whether the information you are viewing is accurate and unbiased.

Useful weblinks

www.emptyhomes.com

www.greenbuildingpress.co.uk

www.greenhouseleeds.co.uk

www.hbf.co.uk

www.housing.org.uk

www.lse.ac.uk

www.moneyadviceservice.org.uk

www.rsnonline.org.uk

www.shelter.org.uk

English housing survey

Key facts from the Headline Report 2011-2012.

⇨ The private rented sector has been growing in recent years, and is at its highest level since the early 1990s, equalling that of the social rented sector at 3.8 million households. In 2011-12, around two-thirds (65%) of households were owner-occupiers.

⇨ Average weekly rents in the private rented sector continued to be well above those in the social rented sector (£164 per week compared with £83). While mean rents have increased in both sectors since 2008-09, private rented sector rents showed no significant change from 2010-11.

⇨ Almost two-thirds (64%) of households in the social rented sector were in receipt of Housing Benefit, compared with around a quarter (26%) of those in the private rented sector.

⇨ There was no significant change in overcrowding rates since 2010-11 for owner occupiers (1%), social renters (7%) or private renters (6%). Rates of under-occupation remained substantially higher in the owner-occupied sector (49%) than in both the social rented sector (10%) and private rented sector (16%).

⇨ The energy efficiency of the housing stock continued to improve: between 1996 and 2011 the average SAP rating of a dwelling increased by 12 SAP points from 45 to 57.

⇨ The proportion of dwellings achieving the highest Energy Efficiency Rating (EER) bands has increased considerably since 1996. In 2011, the social sector had the largest proportion of dwellings in the highest EER Bands A to C (34% of housing association and 26% of local authority dwellings).

⇨ In 2011, 5.4 million dwellings (24%) were non-decent, a reduction of well over 500,000 compared with 2010. The rate was lowest in the social rented sector (17%) and highest in the private rented sector (35%).

⇨ The proportion of dwellings with damp problems has reduced from 13% in 1996 to 5% in 2011. Private rented dwellings were more likely than those in other tenures to experience damp problems, as they were more likely to be older stock.

February 2013

⇨ The above information is reprinted with kind permission from the Department for Communities & Local Government. Please visit www.gov.uk for further information.

People who own their home outright, divided by age-group (2011-12)

Percentage (y-axis) vs Age-group (x-axis):
16-24: sample size too small for reliable estimate
25-34: 1.3%
25-44: 4.1%
45-54: 11.4%
55-64: 24.9%
65+: 58.0%

Source: English Housing Survey, Headline Report 2011-2012, *Department for Communities & Local Government, 2013*

© *Crown copyright 2013*

The locked-out generation

A decade of decline and the deposit gap.

Key findings

The deposit gap

⇨ For those aged between 22 and 29 across England, the average deposit is 229% of net annual salary – in London it is 300%

⇨ For those aged between 30 and 39 across England, the average deposit is 176% of net annual salary – in London it is 232%

A decade of decline

⇨ In 2002 across England it took someone in their twenties putting aside a third of their net income 2.5 years to save a deposit. In 2012 it would take almost seven years.

⇨ In 2002 across England it took someone in their thirties putting aside a third of their net income for two years to save a deposit. In 2012 it would take more than five years.

Across England to reach a deposit:

⇨ 22-29-year-olds need to save 50% of their discretionary monthly income* every month for more than ten years

⇨ 30-39 year olds need to save 50% of their discretionary monthly income every month for six and a half years

Overview

Getting a foot on the property ladder has been something that young people have aspired to for decades. Statistics show that nothing has changed; around 80% of households want to own their own homes. That dream of home ownership has come under severe attack over the last five years and shows little sign of recovery.

This report reveals how difficult it is for young people to get access to home ownership and offers a comparison over the last decade.

First-time buyers are vital to the housing market – they are the drivers of sales in chains across the country and without them transactions slow, the market atrophies. Those who cannot access home-ownership find accommodation in a private rented sector which is being put under increasing pressure. Private rents themselves, having risen over 60% since 1997, are preventing the necessary savings that will enable the security of owner-occupation that most young families crave.

First-time buyers who can't access owner occupancy will also, inevitably, put pressure on social housing which is currently creaking under the weight of existing need – there are 1.7 million families on the social housing waiting list.

Perhaps most worryingly for the long-term future of our country and its economy, our research has revealed that younger generations have put off starting families and pensions as they struggle to save up for a home of their own.

Interest rates, and therefore the costs of servicing mortgages, have remained relatively low but the deposit gap is preventing young people from accessing the housing market. The reduction in lending following the bursting of the credit bubble has meant that the average first-time buyer's deposit is currently 20% of the purchase price. House prices fell during the bursting of the credit bubble but they have remained high in historic terms while the average house price to earnings ratio has also stayed relatively high.

This deposit requirement has locked many first-time buyers out of the housing market with the current average deposit more than £35,000 across England.

Region	Average House Price for First Time Buyer (£) 2012	Deposit needed (£) 2012	Months needed while saving 50% of discretionary income (aged 22-29)	Months needed while saving 50% of discretionary income (aged 30-39)
England	175,265	35,053	126	77
North East	109,180	21,836	74	51
North West	118,722	23,744	83	55
Yorkshire & the Humber	119,078	23,816	78	54
East Midlands	122,217	24,443	82	55
West Midlands	129,332	25,866	91	60
East	172,186	34,437	132	83
London	292,328	58,466	289	128
South East	195,726	39,145	152	88
South West	160,225	32,045	131	86

While we are very clear that there should not be a return to the lax lending practices of the mid-2000s and that it should not be easy to buy a house, this report aims to demonstrate just how difficult it has become for younger generations to buy their first home. As you may expect, we believe that a significant increase in supply over the coming years is vital to solving this affordability and housing crisis.

Home ownership through recent history

Looking back at the last 30 years (see graph opposite) it is possible to see how the environment for first-time buyers has changed dramatically. In 1982, first-time buyer numbers went past 400,000 for the first time ever. Over the next 20 years the number of first time buyers averaged 500,000 annually.

As house prices rose rapidly between 2003 and 2007 the average annual number of first-time buyers fell back to 370,000 and in the last five years that number has been just 198,000.

Meanwhile the size of the deposit needed to get a foot on the ladder has been fairly constant up until the most recent economic crisis. Throughout the 17 years between 1982 and 1998 first-time buyers needed an average of 5% deposit. From 1999 to 2007 that number rose to 10% and since 2008 first-time buyers have on average needed 20% deposits.

Unsurprisingly there is a strong correlation between the average percentage advance and the number of first-time buyers.

February 2013

⇨ The above information is reprinted with kind permission from Home Builders Federation. Please visit www.hbf.co.uk for further information.

© Home Builders Federation 2013

Census shows home ownership drop

Census data from the Office of National Statistics shows that home ownership has fallen for the first time since records began 60 years ago.

Since 2001, home ownership overall has fallen by seven per cent, while the proportion of homes owned with a mortgage has dropped by 15 per cent.

The historic shift reflects the growing trend in young people and families who are unable to get a foot on the property ladder.

Rising numbers are being pushed into the country's rapidly expanding private rental market. The proportion of homes rented privately has rocketed by 69 per cent since 2001.

If current trends continue, the next generation will be bringing up their families in insecure rented housing or at home with their parents. A recent YouGov poll for Shelter revealed that 44 per cent of Britons believe their children or future children won't be able to afford a decent home.

Shelter's chief executive, Campbell Robb, said: 'These figures confirm that home ownership is slipping further and further out of reach, no matter how hard people work or save.

'This means young people are living at home well into their thirties, desperate to get on in life but unable to afford a place of their own.

'Meanwhile, more young families are stuck in rented housing under constant threat of being evicted, worrying about whether they'll have to move again'.

Mr Robb continued: 'Today's broken housing market isn't the result of the credit crunch or mortgage lending, but decades of under-investment in building the affordable homes we need. The Government has got to get a grip on this situation now, otherwise the chances of the next generation getting an affordable home look increasingly bleak.'

5 February 2013

⇨ The above information is reprinted with kind permission from Shelter. Please visit www.shelter.org.uk for further information.

© Shelter 2013

Housing: are we creating a new bubble?

By John Humphrys

John Humphrys asks: are we at last pulling out of recession? Or are we simply seeing the inflating of a bubble that one day will burst?

Rising house prices are often seen as a sign that an economy is picking up. That's certainly how things look in the United States at the moment where the cost of a house has risen over ten percent in the last year and economic optimism has lifted accordingly. Here in Britain house prices are also on the rise, at the fastest rate for six years. So does this mean we're at last pulling out of recession? Or are we simply seeing the inflating of a bubble that one day will burst?

One of the features of the 'Great Recession', as the economic dumps of the last few years have come to be known, was that the housing market essentially went dead. The building of new houses virtually ground to a halt despite the fact that the need for new houses, especially to accommodate younger first-time buyers, was and remains so great. At the same time anyone wanting to raise a mortgage found it next to impossible. Traumatised banks, still smarting from the effects of being ready to lend almost anything to almost anyone during the boom years, became unwilling to stump up new loans. The deposits they required in order to grant a mortgage became prohibitive for many people, especially first-time buyers.

The result was that house prices nationally (though not everywhere) fell, although not anything like enough to restore historic levels of affordability. The ratio of average house prices to average earnings remained far too high for many people to think of buying a flat or a house even if they could raise the loan.

The Government's approach to extricating Britain from the Great Recession while pursuing an austerity policy to reduce its own debts has been to encourage the Bank of England to flood the place with money. This increased liquidity has had a predictable effect on asset prices with both the bond markets and the stock markets rising appreciably. It's also had an effect on the housing market.

Figures released this month showed that nationally house prices in March were 2.7% higher than a year before. In London the figure was 7.6% and in certain parts of the capital (not just the rich boroughs like Kensington and Chelsea, so attractive to rich Russian oligarchs) the rise was in double figures.

Part of the cause of this rise in prices has been deliberate Government action to stimulate the housing market. Its Funding for Lending Scheme subsidised the cost of mortgages in an attempt to end the stand-off between unwilling lenders and potential buyers desperate to find ways to finance their house-buying ambitions.

In his Budget in March the Chancellor went further, announcing a new 'Help to Buy Scheme' to come into effect next January. This will provide help with equity loans for purchases of newly-built houses – a policy aimed at stimulating more new house-building. But the policy will also provide up to £130 billion in state guarantees for up to 20% of the purchase price of a house to would-be home owners with only small deposits at their disposal. This is intended to encourage lenders to provide finance to this large group of potential borrowers, many of them young.

The Government knows that part of the problem with the housing market is the shortage of supply, especially of new houses. In addition to these measures it is trying to lighten planning laws so that it will be easier for house-builders to build. Inevitably, though, such a policy encounters opposition so the effect on supply is likely to be delayed, at the very least.

In such a context many commentators are worried that Government action on the demand side can have only one effect – a rise in prices, the very thing we are already seeing.

The simple economics of supply and demand tells us that if demand is increased without any matching increase in supply, then prices will rise. Furthermore, the very fact of announcing a policy not due to come into effect until next year creates an anticipation of rising prices so bringing them forward.

The government has not lacked critics warning it of the dangers it may be running. Last week, in its annual assessment of the British economy, the International Monetary Fund cast doubt on the idea that the government's measures would lead to an increase in the supply of houses. Instead, it said, "the result would ultimately be mostly house price increases that would work against the aim of boosting housing access".

The outgoing governor of the Bank of England, Sir Mervyn King, has been even more outspoken, saying of the Help to Buy Scheme: "There is no place in the long run for a scheme of this kind."

In its defence the Government points out that its stated intention is for the scheme to run only for three years. But there is some uncertainty as to whether it's intended that the Government itself or the Bank will have the responsibility for ultimately blowing the whistle on the scheme. And history suggests that it is very difficult for governments to extricate themselves from policies that subsidise house purchase because of the perceived unfairness to people who come too late to benefit from the subsidy. It took decades for governments finally to abandon mortgage interest tax relief.

Cynics point out that in the meantime it is in the government's electoral interests to see house prices rise because the 'feelgood factor' tends to rise with it, at least among those lucky enough already to own their own homes (disproportionately Conservative and LibDem voters).

But the wider effect of rising house prices is dire, they say. Making houses even more expensive simply redistributes wealth from the already impecunious young to the already well-heeled middle-aged and old. Furthermore, higher house prices encourage those who already own their homes to remortgage them in order to finance ordinary consumption – in other words, to borrow more in order to take an additional foreign holiday, exactly the sort of debt-fuelled consumption that characterised the last boom before it went bust. And finally, critics say, government guarantees of mortgage loans will encourage banks and other lenders to engage in riskier lending than they would otherwise be prepared to do – yet another feature of the bubble that got us into the current mess.

To these criticisms the government would no doubt say that they really do regard the policy as temporary and that it is necessary if the housing market is not going to remain in the doldrums forever. Furthermore, they argue, their policy is targeted on young, first-time buyers who would otherwise be without hope of getting on the housing ladder unless they were lucky enough to have rich parents. And they say they really are doing all they can to get house-building going again, so easing the pressure on prices.

So is it the right policy? Or are we just repeating an old mistake and blowing up a bubble that is bound to burst?

29 May 2012

⇨ The above information is reprinted with kind permission from YouGov Plc. Please visit www.yougov.co.uk for further information.

First time buyers: richer and… younger?

Figures out yesterday showed that the cost of buying a home in London rose on average £28,000 last year. That's a yearly rise equivalent to the average London income. No wonder renters feel that the dream of home ownership is out of reach.

The Land Registry data also indicates another trend: younger first time buyers.

Across England and Wales the number of properties sold for under £200,000 fell by 7% over the last year, while the number of properties sold for over £1 million increased by 14%.

In London, where prices are rising fastest, there was a 25% increase in homes sold for over £1 million while the number sold for under £300,000 fell by 9%.

Does this mean that there has been a huge decline in first time buyers?

No. According to mortgage lenders, the number of homes bought by first time buyers has been increasing in recent months. Even as homes become less affordable for those on ordinary incomes, the number of first time buyers is increasing.

This is a conundrum. The number of first time buyers is rising (from the very low levels we saw during the recession) but the number of properties sold at traditional first time buyer prices is falling rapidly. How can this be?

The answer, I believe, is that we are seeing a shift in the sort of people who are becoming first time buyers. The Council of Mortgage Lenders (CML) have collated data showing that it is increasingly likely, especially in London, that first time buyers will have massive parental help. So it seems that the growth in first time buyers is coming from people with help from wealthy parents, who are buying more expensive properties than 'traditional' first time buyers. Other areas of growth, especially in the capital, are from foreign investors and buy to let landlords.

This effect might also explain an anomaly: despite the widespread belief that the average age of a first time buyer is rising into the late 30s, in actual fact it's still steady at 29.

As CML demonstrate, the key difference is between unassisted and assisted first time buyers. Unsurprisingly, 'real' first timers who saved up themselves are older than those with big deposits provided for them. But although the savers are getting older, they are also getting fewer, which is presumably why the average age of all first time buyers hasn't changed.

If prices continue to outstrip wages and the ability to save, they will become rarer still. At some point, the average age of a first time buyer may start to be dragged down by this effect, even as house prices rise.

What all this means is that we may reach the bizarre situation where house prices become less obtainable, but first time buyers start getting younger on average. If any drop in the average age of a first time buyer does happen, it's bound to lead to claims that the housing crisis is finally over.

Of course, what's really happening is that ordinary families on middle incomes are being squeezed out – leaving just the lucky few who can depend on the Bank of Mum and Dad.

20 January 2013

⇨ The above information is reprinted with kind permission from Shelter. Please visit www.shelter.org.uk for further information.

Should you rent or buy?

Buying a property is probably the biggest financial decision you'll ever have to make. How do you know whether it's the right decision for you right now – or whether you'd be better off renting instead?

the **Money Advice Service**®

Things to weigh up if you're not sure whether to buy or rent

Owning your own home is a huge commitment, not just to the building you buy and the area you choose to live in, but also to your life (and to another person if you are buying with a loved one or friend).

Benefits of owning your home

⇨ There are many benefits to home ownership. Here are just some of them.

⇨ Once you've paid off your mortgage, your home will be yours and it could be worth far more than you paid for it.

⇨ If your home increases in value you can use that equity to help you afford a bigger home or to fund a more comfortable retirement if you downsize.

⇨ When you retire you won't necessarily have the income you need to keep on paying rent – if you have paid your mortgage off you'll be living there 'rent free'.

⇨ You can spend money improving your home and increasing its value, whereas you can't alter a rented home without the landlord's permission.

⇨ Sometimes it can be cheaper to buy than to rent.

Potential downsides of owning

⇨ It's a big financial commitment – you need to be sure you can afford what you're taking on. See the later section 'Can you afford to buy?'

⇨ You also need to be sure you can afford maintenance costs such as replacing a boiler if it packs up or fixing a leaky roof. If you stretch yourself too much when you buy you may resent not having money for meals out, holidays and entertainment.

⇨ You have less flexibility than when renting. For example, if you want to move for work or personal reasons, selling up and moving on is far more expensive if you own as you'll have all of the associated estate agency and legal fees. Also bear in mind that it may not always be easy to sell your home – you'll be dependent on what's happening in the market.

⇨ If you're living with someone else and split up, the process of sorting out the property will be far more complicated and expensive.

Are you better off buying or renting?

You're not necessarily going to be better off financially buying rather than renting your home.

If the value of your property falls, you may find yourself unable to sell because you owe more to your mortgage lender than your home is worth.

On the other hand, if house prices rise, you could make a nice profit that could help fund a move to a bigger home or give you a lump sum if you choose to downsize later on in life.

You can use the Rent or Buy calculator on the Green Gem website to work out whether you are better off buying or renting.

Can you afford to buy?

The first step towards buying a property is figuring out whether you can afford to do so. There are many costs associated with buying your own home, beyond your mortgage repayments, including:

⇨ deposit

⇨ legal costs such as solicitor's fees

⇨ survey cost

⇨ Stamp Duty

⇨ removal costs, and

⇨ your monthly bills – such as gas, electricity, home phone, etc.

If buying isn't an option for you right now, think about setting up a savings plan to achieve your goal in the future.

Affordable home schemes if you're on a low income

If you're on a low income, are trying to buy your first home or are a key worker there are several schemes available that allow you to part-rent/part-buy a home with a view to buying it outright gradually over time. In England there's also a scheme to help with first-time buyer deposits.

⇨ The above information is reprinted with kind permission from The Money Advice Service. Please visit www.moneyadviceservice.org.uk for further information.

Home ownership schemes

You may be able to get financial help through a Help to Buy home ownership scheme if you live in England and can't afford to buy a home. (Wales and Scotland have different schemes.)

The four types of Help to Buy scheme are:

⇨ Help to Buy equity loans

⇨ shared ownership

⇨ NewBuy

⇨ Help to Buy mortgage guarantees – available from January 2014.

There are also schemes for council and housing association tenants. Read the guides on Right to Buy and Right to Acquire.

Help to Buy equity loans

Help to Buy equity loans are open to both first-time buyers and home movers on new-build homes worth up to £600,000.

You won't be able to sub-let your home if you use this scheme.

How it works

With a Help to Buy equity loan:

⇨ you'll need to contribute at least 5% of the property price as a deposit

⇨ the government will give you a loan for up to 20% of the price

⇨ you'll need a mortgage of up to 75% to cover the rest

Example

For a property worth £200,000	Amount	Percentage
Cash deposit	£10,000	5%
Equity loan	£40,000	20%
Your mortgage	£150,000	75%

If the home in the table above sold for £210,000, you'd get £168,000 (80%, from your mortgage and the cash deposit) and pay back £42,000 on the loan (20%). You'd need to pay off your mortgage with your share of the money.

Equity loan fees

You won't be charged loan fees for the first five years of owning your home.

In the sixth year, you'll be charged a fee of 1.75% of the loan's value. After this, the fee will increase every year. The increase is worked out by using the Retail Prices Index plus 1%.

Your Help to Buy agent will contact you before the fees start, to set up monthly payments with your bank.

You'll also be sent a statement about your loan each year.

Fees don't count towards paying back the equity loan.

Applying for an equity loan

Contact the Help to Buy agent in the area you want to live if you'd like to buy a home with an equity loan.

Selling your home and paying back the loan

The home will be in your name, which means you can sell it at any time. You'll have to pay back the equity loan when you sell your home or at the end of your mortgage period – whichever comes first.

You can also pay back some of your equity loan without selling your home. You can pay back either 10% or 20% or the total amount, so long as the loan is worth at least 10% of the value of your home.

Talk to your lender and Help to Buy agent if you want to pay the loan back in full.

Shared ownership schemes

Shared ownership schemes are provided through housing associations. You buy a share of your home (between 25% and 75% of the home's value) and pay rent on the remaining share.

You'll need to take out a mortgage to pay for your share of the home's purchase price.

Shared ownership properties are always leasehold.

Eligibility

You can buy a home through shared ownership if:

⇨ your household earns £60,000 a year or less

⇨ you're a first-time buyer (or you used to own a home, but can't afford to buy one now)

⇨ you rent a council or housing association property.

Older people

You can get help from another Help to Buy scheme called 'Older People's Shared Ownership' if you're aged 55 or over.

It works in the same way as the general shared ownership scheme, but you can only buy up to 75% of your home. Once you own 75% you won't have to pay rent on the remaining share.

People with disabilities

Home Ownership for People with Long-Term Disabilities (HOLD) can help you buy any home that's for sale on a shared ownership basis if you have a long-term disability.

You can only apply for HOLD if the properties available in the other Help to Buy schemes don't meet your needs, e.g. you need a ground-floor

property. Your local Help to Buy agent can help you.

Buying more shares

You can buy more shares in your home any time after you become the owner. This is known as staircasing.

The cost of your new share will depend on how much your home is worth when you want to buy the share. If property prices in your area have gone up, you'll pay more than for your first share. If your home has dropped in value, your new share will be cheaper.

The housing association will get the property valued and let you know the cost of your new share. You'll have to pay the valuer's fee.

Selling your home

If you own 100% of your home, you can sell it yourself. When you put it up for sale, the housing association has the right to buy the property back first. This is known as 'first refusal' and the housing association has this right for 21 years after you fully own the home.

If you own a share of your home, the housing association has the right to find a buyer for it.

NewBuy

NewBuy lets you buy a newly built home with a deposit of only 5% of the purchase price.

Who qualifies?

To qualify for NewBuy, your new home must be:

⇨ a new build – being sold for the first time or for the first time in its current form (e.g. a new flat that used to be part of a house)

⇨ priced £500,000 or less

⇨ your main home (you can't use NewBuy to buy a second home or a buy-to-let property)

⇨ owned fully by you (you can't use NewBuy for shared ownership or shared equity purchases)

⇨ built by a builder taking part in the scheme

To qualify you must be either:

⇨ a UK citizen

⇨ someone with the right to remain indefinitely in the UK.

You don't have to be a first-time buyer and there's no limit on your level of income. But you can't use NewBuy with any other publicly funded mortgage scheme.

How to apply

You apply for a mortgage from an approved lender. The lender will check that you can afford to repay it, as they would for any other type of mortgage.

You could get a mortgage of up to 95% of the purchase price if the lender is satisfied and you meet all the criteria above.

Help to Buy mortgage guarantees

From 1 January 2014, the Help to Buy mortgage guarantee will help you buy a home with a deposit of only 5% of the purchase price.

Help to Buy mortgage guarantees will be open to both first-time buyers and home movers. However, you won't be able to get a Help to Buy mortgage guarantee if you're planning on renting out the property.

The guarantee is provided to your lender – not to you.

Eligibility

To qualify for a Help to Buy mortgage guarantee, the home you want to buy must:

⇨ be offered for sale at £600,000 or less

⇨ not be a shared ownership or shared equity purchase.

The property can be newly built or already existing.

You don't have to be a first-time buyer and there's no limit on your level of income. But you can't use Help to Buy with any other publicly funded mortgage scheme. More information will be available later in 2013.

⇨ The above information is reprinted with kind permission from GOV.UK. Please visit www.gov.uk for further information.

© Crown copyright 2013

Should we get Help to Buy or save for a bigger house deposit?

We have a big enough deposit if we use the Help to Buy scheme, but have read so many negative articles about it.

By Virginia Wallis

Q. *I am a 25-year-old teacher and live in Kent with my boyfriend who is a PhD student. We rent a shoe box at a cost of £600 a month, which allows us to save towards a deposit to buy a house. It will soon be enough if we were to buy using the Government's Help to Buy scheme. However, I have read so many articles about the negatives of this policy I am doubting whether this is a good idea. My question is, should we buy a house now with only a 5% deposit and accept government help, or should we wait? Saving for a 10% deposit will probably take us another five years, and we are keen to start a family in our own home – but I'd rather wait if the financial implications of using Help to Buy are very risky.*

A. There are two main criticisms levelled at the government's Help to Buy scheme, which was announced in this year's budget. First, that it will push up house prices, thus making property even less affordable to people trying to get a foot on the property ladder. The second criticism is that because it encourages people to take out a loan equivalent to 95% of the value of a property – made up of a 75% loan from a lender and 20% from government – borrowers will be at risk of negative equity if property prices subsequently fall, especially if they buy at an inflated price in the first place. Negative equity is where your property is worth less than the amount of your mortgage, meaning you wouldn't be able to pay off the loan if you sold the property.

However, negative equity is a problem only if you want to move or remortgage, so if you plan to be in the property for some time the possibility of being in negative equity may be a risk you are prepared to take.

The advantage of using the Help to Buy scheme is that for the first five years of the loan you pay no interest on it. After the five years are up you will pay a fee of 1.75% of the loan, which will increase every year by 1% plus RPI. However, you are also allowed to pay the government loan back early, thus increasing the amount of the property you own and reducing the risk of negative equity. You can either pay off the whole lot or instalments of either 10% or 20% of the total amount.

So instead of waiting the five years you say it will take you to save up for a 10% deposit, you could buy now using Help to Buy and use those five years to save up enough to pay off a portion – or all – of the government loan before you have to start paying the post-five-year fees. It's also worth noting that if the Help to Buy scheme really does inflate house prices, by waiting five years before you buy you run the risk of not actually being able to save enough for a 10% deposit, because you'll need a bigger amount than you now need.

But one big question you need to answer is: do you want to buy a new-build home? If you don't, the current Help to Buy scheme is not for you, as it only applies to new-build properties. However, provided you have a deposit of 5%, both new and older properties will be eligible for help when the second leg of the Help to Buy initiative is introduced in January 2014.

It is slightly different from the current scheme in that rather than granting you an interest-free loan, the Government guarantees 15% of your mortgage. This is supposed to encourage lenders to provide bigger mortgages than they normally would to someone with a 5% deposit. But the Government can't guarantee that taking out a 95% mortgage doesn't run the risk of someone falling into negative equity.

Finally, nothing in either of the Help to Buy schemes changes lenders' mortgage lending criteria, so depending on how your boyfriend's studies are funded, the fact that he is a PhD student may work against you when getting a mortgage. But If you are planning to apply for a mortgage on your earnings alone, this shouldn't be a problem.

12 June 2013

More people rent homes privately

More households are renting their homes privately in England than living in social housing for the first time since the 1960s, government figures show.

Meanwhile, the proportion of households who own their home has slumped to its lowest level in 25 years as the private rental sector has boomed, the English Housing Survey 2011-12 showed.

The figures reflect the strong levels of demand in the rental sector as many people have found themselves locked out of home ownership in the tough economy.

Some 17.4% or 3.84 million households were living in the private rental sector last year, compared with 17.3% or 3.80 million renting from councils or housing associations. The vast majority of households are home owners, making up 14.39 million, but at 65.3% of households this is the lowest proportion recorded since 1987.

The survey also found an increase in the proportion of households within the private rental sector which are classed as overcrowded, meaning that the number of bedrooms is not enough to avoid some 'undesirable sharing'.

The proportion of overcrowded households in the private rental sector has doubled from 3% in the mid-1990s to 6% in 2011-12. Around three-fifths of private renters, equating to 2.2 million households, said that they expected to buy a property at some point in the future – but 45% thought it would be five years or more before they did so.

Campbell Robb, chief executive of charity Shelter, said the figures are 'bad news for anyone struggling to find a decent and affordable home'. He said: 'As saving for a home of their own becomes increasingly out of reach, many have no choice but to live in rented homes for years on end. Today's figures take the growth of 'generation rent' to a whole new level. This should be the wake-up call that the Government needs to make renting fit for purpose.'

In 1961, there were 3.2 million households living in social housing, while 4.7 million lived in the private rental sector. But a decade later this had been reversed and by 1971 there were 4.6 million families living in social housing compared with 3.2 million who were privately renting.

Shelter recently produced a report which argued that the private rental sector has outgrown its role in primarily providing accommodation for students and young professionals. The charity said that families have become stuck in the 'rent trap' as rents have soared due to strong demand, which has left tenants with little cash to be able to save for a mortgage deposit.

A spokesman for the Department for Communities and Local Government said: 'The revamped Right to Buy is also providing a boost to aspiring homeowners, offering 2.5 million social tenants the opportunity to buy their home with discounts of up to £75,000. These measures have resulted in the highest number of first-time buyers since 2007 and affordability for first-time buyers is the best it has been since 2003.'

8 February 2013

⇨ The above information is reprinted with kind permission from AOL Money & Finance. Please visit www.money.aol.co.uk for further information.

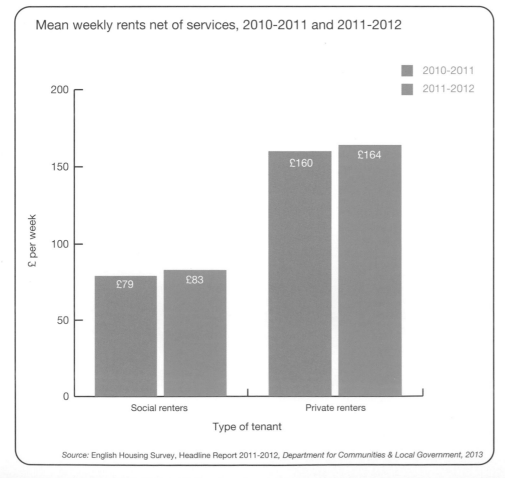

Mean weekly rents net of services, 2010-2011 and 2011-2012

- 2010-2011
- 2011-2012

£ per week

Social renters: £79, £83
Private renters: £160, £164

Type of tenant

Source: English Housing Survey, Headline Report 2011-2012, *Department for Communities & Local Government, 2013*

Reform is needed to protect tenants from rogue landlords as renting soars

Checks need to be in place to ensure standards rise alongside the growth in demand for rented housing.

London's private rented sector has changed. One in four Londoners now rents privately, and the sector ballooned by 75% over the decade to 2011.

However, despite numerous government reviews and third sector campaigns, the policy and regulatory approach remains stuck in the 1980s.

In a new report from the London Assembly, we make the case for change to the rented market. A shortage of social and council housing, mixed with runaway house prices, means more Londoners than ever before believe owning their own home is a distant dream.

Reform is now needed so tenants aren't at risk from rogue landlords – a small sector of the market – whose interests lie solely in their keenness to line their pockets at the expense of their tenants.

Demand for rented housing exceeds supply to the point that now landlords can continue to raise rents without improving standards.

This is a £13 billion-a-year business in London and growing. A package of tough measures is needed to improve the way the sector functions. We're championing reforms including rent stabilisation, longer tenancies, higher penalties and landlord registration. But we believe honest landlords should not fear these reforms.

Regardless of rogue landlords, there are other pressing reasons for reform. If the Government continues to use the private sector as a substitute for social housing, security and better conditions for tenants must become part of the deal. Government would also see the benefits of rent stabilisation in the form of reduced housing benefits.

It's ludicrous to say these reforms will only harm landlords. As well as making the sector more credible, the report makes the strong point that landlords – those who act within the rules – should be rewarded. Registered landlords could access local authority services at a reduced price to lower their running costs and help guarantee a steady stream of tenants. The Residential Landlords Association (RLA) reacted negatively to our report, expressing concern that the committee wanted to see a return to the past by calling for rent stabilisation, which they believed would 'cause untold damage to the housing market, with tenants losing out'.

We are not seeking old-style rent controls. What we are looking for is a sustainable way of allowing landlords to make a profit while also making rises more stable and predictable for tenants by linking them to an index. This seems a fairer and more transparent system, and evidence suggests it works.

Increases in line with inflation work well in mainland Europe, creating much larger and better functioning private rented sectors than we currently enjoy in London. It is also just one recommendation in a package of reforms that will make it easier – and probably cheaper – for landlords to run their businesses.

We are open to debate about how rent stabilisation could work. Mayor Boris Johnson should use the expertise and finances at his disposal to test the feasibility of rent stabilisation in a London pilot.

Shelter reports nearly half of London's renters have only £100 or less disposable income once essentials such as rent, fuel bills, food and council tax have been paid. Can it be right that so many Londoners have so little left after paying their rent?

I believe those who argue vehemently against reforms that will empower tenants and improve standards, convinced they will lead to a catastrophic loss of homes in London, are wrong. Only a foolish landlord would pack it in while the market is so profitable. Instead, hard-pressed tenants might question how most other western economies can have a better regulated sector, while also enjoying a larger and more affordable rental market.

Measures must be taken to make it far more difficult for rogue landlords to profit from sub-standard letting in London.

Len Duvall chaired the Assembly's investigation and is the Labour London Assembly member for Greenwich and Lewisham.

12 June 2013

⇨ The above article is reprinted with kind permission from *The Guardian*. Please visit www. guardian.co.uk for further information.

© 2013 Guardian News and Media Limited

WELL, IT IS WITHIN OUR PRICE RANGE!

What is social housing?

Social housing is housing that is let at low rents and on a secure basis to people in housing need. It is generally provided by councils and not-for-profit organisations such as housing associations.

Social housing provides affordable housing

A key function of social housing is to provide accommodation that is affordable to people on low incomes. Rents in the social housing sector are kept low through state subsidy. The social housing sector is currently governed by a strictly defined system of rent control to ensure that rents are kept affordable.

Social housing is allocated on the basis of need

Unlike the private rental sector, in which tenancies are offered according to the free choice of the landlord or existing household in question, social housing is allocated according to need.

Each social landlord operates an allocations policy, stating in advance what factors will be taken into account when deciding who gets preference for the limited amount of social housing

on offer. These policies must include 'reasonable preference criteria' that are set out in law, but beyond this, allocations policies can be drawn up at the discretion of the social landlord.

Social housing is owned and managed by social landlords

Social landlords are the bodies that own and manage social housing. They tend to be non-commercial organisations such as local authorities or housing associations. Housing associations are independent, not-for-profit organisations that use any surpluses they generate to maintain existing homes and to help finance new ones. It is now possible for commercial organisations to build and manage social housing, although this is not yet common practice.

Social housing is tightly regulated

Social housing and landlords are tightly regulated. The Government

department currently responsible for overseeing the social housing sector is Communities and Local Government (CLG). CLG has direct oversight of local authority housing. Housing associations are funded by the Government through the Homes and Communities Agency, which is responsible for the construction of new social homes.

Shelter's view

Shelter believes that any definition of social housing must include the requirement for all social housing to offer:

⇨ low rents affordable for people working on the minimum wage

⇨ security of tenure for life.

Who gets social housing?

The question of who gets and who doesn't get social housing provokes heated discussion.

Overall, 18 per cent of all households in England live in social housing.[1] Among them, however, households with certain characteristics are over-represented:

⇨ single parents: 44 per cent of lone parents live in social housing.[2]

⇨ older people: 21 per cent of people over 65 live in social housing, 24 per cent of people aged 75 or over live in social housing.[3]

⇨ ethnic minorities: 26 per cent of ethnic minority households live in social housing.[4]

⇨ economically inactive: 60 per cent of social housing tenants are economically inactive (31 per cent

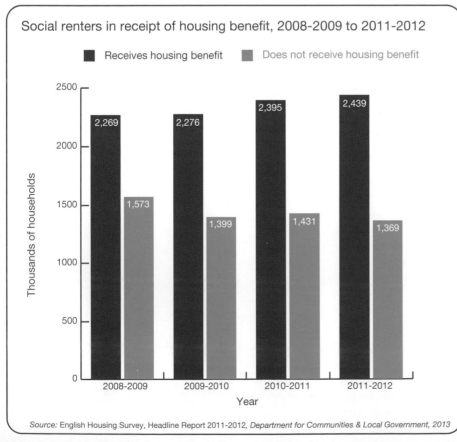

Social renters in receipt of housing benefit, 2008-2009 to 2011-2012

■ Receives housing benefit   ■ Does not receive housing benefit

Source: English Housing Survey, Headline Report 2011-2012, *Department for Communities & Local Government, 2013*

1 Survey of English Housing, Preliminary Report: 2007/08, CLG, 2009.

2 Ibid.

3 Housing Statistics 2008, CLG, 2009

4 Survey of English Housing, Preliminary Report: 2007/08, CLG, 2009.

are retired and 29 per cent are otherwise economically inactive).[5]

⇨ unemployed: six per cent of social housing tenants are unemployed.[6]

There are also large numbers of disabled people, and people on housing benefit living in social housing. Vulnerable groups are concentrated in the social housing sector, where there are low rates of employment and low income levels:

⇨ The median gross income for households in social housing in 2007/08 was £10,900, compared with £23,320 for households across all tenures.[7] 44 per cent of households in social housing have an annual income of less than £10,000.[8]

⇨ Only seven per cent of all households in social housing have a gross annual income of £30,000 or above.[9]

How is social housing allocated?

The main factors that determine whether an individual or family is offered social housing are:

⇨ availability of social housing: this varies throughout the country – for example, in London and the South East demand for social housing massively outstrips supply.

⇨ eligibility: to be offered social housing, an applicant must be eligible to apply. People will not be eligible for an allocation if they are subject to immigration control (i.e. they require permission to enter or remain in the UK), or they do have a right to live in the UK but have recently returned to the UK after spending a significant amount of time living abroad.

In some cases, an applicant may also be ineligible for an allocation if

the local authority believes that any member of their household is guilty of unacceptable behaviour that is serious enough to make her/him unsuitable to be a council tenant.

Housing allocation policies

All local authorities are free to set their own housing allocation policy as long as it conforms to certain legal guidelines. By law, local authorities must clearly set out procedures and priorities by which social housing will be allocated and ensure that information on these policies is made publicly available. Local authorities must also ensure that the following groups are given 'reasonable preference' under any allocation scheme:

⇨ people who are legally classed as homeless (or threatened with homelessness): the law classes a person as homeless when they have no home that is available and reasonable to occupy

⇨ people occupying unsanitary, overcrowded or otherwise unsatisfactory housing

⇨ people who need to move for medical or welfare reasons

⇨ people who need to move to a particular location: for example, to be nearer to special training opportunities or special medical facilities and who would suffer hardship if they were unable to do so.

Most local authorities operate points-based systems, taking into account how long applicants have been on a waiting list for social housing (officially known as a housing register), their level of housing need, and other designated priorities.

Housing associations operate their own waiting lists and lettings policies, although they are expected to make a proportion of their lettings available to applicants approved by local authorities.

⇨ The above information is reprinted with kind permission from Shelter. Please visit www.shelter.org.uk for further information.

© Shelter 2013

5 Ibid.

6 Survey of English Housing, Preliminary Report: 2007/08, CLG, 2009.

7 Data supplied by CLG, 2009.

8 Family Resources Survey, DWP.

9 Ibid.

Bedroom Tax evictions begin with vulnerable residents saying they feel 'victimised'

The first evictions over the government's controversial "bedroom tax" are set to begin as notices and final demand letters are being put through the letter boxes of social housing tenants around the country.

A man suffering from acute depression and a grandmother with sciatica are both facing eviction, with Scotland's council being one of the first to crack down on arrears.

Jane McClements, 59, who was told to pay £17.33 a week more, told the Daily Record she couldn't find the money. She added that she needs the spare room so that when her sciatica flares up her husband can sleep in a separate bed.

"I feel like we are being victimised," she told the paper.

"It is nothing more than a tax on the poorest people in society."

Alan from Lanarkshire, who did not want to tell the Daily Mirror his full name, suffers from acute depression. He had a nervous breakdown in 2003 and his mother died by suicide.

He didn't even want two bedrooms but at the time he moved into social housing officials said there were no one bed houses available.

The High Court has already been asked to declare that the government's so-called "bedroom tax" unlawfully discriminates against disabled people, in 10 cases brought to illustrate the serious impact of the regulations up and down the country.

One of the claimants lives with her husband in a two-bedroom housing association flat in Stockport.

She is severely disabled with Spina Bifida and has to sleep in a fixed position in a hospital bed with an electronic pressure mattress.

Another claimant is disabled widower Richard Rourke, with three bedrooms, who is now building up rent arrears.

He has a disabled stepdaughter at university who suffers from a rare form of muscular dystrophy and needs one of the rooms when she comes home during holidays and at weekends.

The other room is a box room he uses to store essential equipment, including a hoist for lifting him, a power chair and shower seat.

Another applicant, James Daly, from Stoke, is the father of a severely-disabled son who stays with him every weekend and at least one day during the week, as well as part of the school holidays, and when his mother is away.

Separated from his wife, Mr Daly occupies a two-bedroom flat but is deemed to be over-occupying the property by one bedroom - his son's room.

Bedroom tax might actually be costing the country more too, with figures revealing the introduction of the "spare room subsidy" has seen the number of people claiming extra handouts from councils to meet housing costs soar.

More than 25,000 people applied for discretionary housing payments (DHP) to help cover their rent in April, compared with 5,700 in the same month last year, according to an analysis of 51 councils by The Independent.

Councillor John Cotton, cabinet member for equalities, told the newspaper: "It's a situation like the 1930s here in Birmingham.

"We are a city that has a hill to climb in terms of deprivation. With the impact of changes like this, the hill just got even steeper. It's putting more and more pressure on vulnerable communities."

A grandmother who killed herself earlier in May blamed the bedroom tax for her death.

Stephanie Bottrill, who killed herself earlier this month, wrote in her final letter: "I don't [blame] anyone for me death expect [sic] the government."

Just days before she died, the 53-year-old, from in Solihull in the West Midlands, told neighbours she simply could not afford to live any more.

Her family told the Sunday People she was tortured about how she would afford the £20 extra a week for the two under-occupied bedrooms in her home - money she owed because of the government's spare room subsidy policy, the so-called "bedroom tax."

A Department of Work and Pensions (DWP) spokesman said officials were "monitoring" the situation to ensure that those who needed support received it.

The new regulations, introduced on April 1, led to reductions in housing benefit payments to social tenants assessed to be under-occupying their accommodation.

22 May 2013

⇨ The above information is reprinted with kind permission from *The Huffington Post UK*. Please visit www.huffingtonpost.co.uk for further information.

Poll: are lifetime social tenancies an outdated policy?

One London council has scrapped lifetime tenancies for new social housing applicants, branding the historic policy 'antiquated' and 'unfair'. Do you agree?

A London council has scrapped lifetime tenancies for new social housing applicants.

The London Borough of Hammersmith & Fulham will now only offer five-year tenancies to new applicants, reduced to two years for residents aged between 18 and 25 or who have a history of antisocial behaviour.

The council will also prioritise applications for working households with a connection to the borough, as well as ex-service personnel and foster carers. Existing tenancies in the borough will be unaffected by the changes.

Under the new allocations policy, households earning more than £40,200 will be blocked from registering on the council's housing waiting list and redirected towards low-cost home ownership instead.

Previously, social tenants enjoyed lifetime tenancy agreements with the rights to the property passing on to the next generation. Councils were given licence to offer flexible tenancies and granted greater discretion over waiting lists in 2010 by former housing minister Grant Shapps.

Andrew Johnson, the council's cabinet member for housing, described the former system as unfair and antiquated and said it created disadvantaged communities:

'We believe that the notion of a tenancy for life is outdated and that it is wrong to expect to inherit a welfare benefit in the form of a heavily subsidised house irrespective of housing need.

'We also think that it is patently unfair that people can move to this borough from other parts of the country or even further afield and access social housing ahead of hard-working local residents who have been living here for many years.

'The old, antiquated system has created disadvantaged communities by producing concentrations of people on benefits with disproportionately high levels of unemployment and sometimes social breakdown.

'In its place, we want to create neighbourhoods where a broad mix of social households all live side-by-side.'

Are lifetime social housing tenancies an outdated idea?

6 March 2013

⇨ The above article is reprinted with kind permission from *The Guardian*. Please visit www.guardian.co.uk for further information.

The UK's housing crises

Reduced demand during the recession has been reflected in falling house prices outside London and the South East and a slump in construction everywhere. Data from the Department for Communities and Local Government show that between their peak in 2007 and 2011, house prices fell by 12% in the North East and by 10% in the North West. Between September 2011 and September 2012, land registry data show further price falls of 3.2% in the North East and 2.2% in the North West.

There has also been a severe slump in construction in these parts of the country. In the North East, construction (measured as permanent dwellings completed) has fallen by 36% from its 2007/08 peak. In the North West, construction has fallen by 47%.

Prices have held up much better in London and the South East. A large initial fall in London (9.3%) was quickly offset by subsequent rises, leading to an overall increase of 3.8% between 2007 and 2011. The South East saw a similar initial fall and a slightly weaker recovery, but prices still increased by 1.4% between 2007 and 2011. Between September 2011 and September 2012, land registry data show a continued recovery with prices rising by 5.5% in London and by 2.3% in the South East.

Despite these different price trajectories, construction has still slumped, even if the impact is somewhat less pronounced: 12% down from the peak for London; and 19% down from the peak for the South East.

While we should not downplay short-term concerns about the impact of falling house prices on consumer demand, it is the construction figures that are most worrying. The UK's more profound housing crisis is the overall shortage of housing and the problems of affordability that this generates (see, for example, Hilber and Vermeulen, 2012).

These problems, already acute in the South East, can only be exacerbated by recent trends of slow income growth, falling construction and rising prices. Even with the general price falls in Northern regions, affordability remains a problem for the more successful cities, such as Manchester.

Focusing on the short-run slump also distracts from the longer-run problem that the UK was building very few houses even during the good times. At the height of the boom, England was building 170,000 new homes a year. The annual average between 1998 and 2007 was 150,000 new homes.

To put these numbers in perspective, note that between 2001 and 2011, about 1.4 million new homes were built in England, while the population rose by just under four million. With an average household size of a little over two people per household, it is not surprising that prices rose so sharply. The now defunct National Housing and Planning Advice Unit suggested that we would need to build around 270,000 homes a year just to stabilise (not reduce) prices.

Managing the demand for housing

So what can be done? Some have called for the problem to be tackled 'head-on' by rent control measures to restrict rising prices. That would be great for people who get rent-controlled houses, awful for everyone else. In the long run, it would also massively distort the rental sector (because it reduces the returns to renting and increases the cost of moving). Quite simply, this is a very bad option.

AFFORDABILITY

Instead of intervening directly to control prices, an alternative set of measures aims to intervene on the demand side of the housing market. These measures are of two broad kinds. The first seeks to dampen demand; for example, through changes in the way in which housing is taxed. Subjecting housing to capital gains taxes would be a good if very unpopular example.

To the extent that these arguments are about reducing the pro-cyclicality of the housing market (the tendency for demand to rise very rapidly as the economy booms), there is something to recommend them. It is less clear to what extent they would solve the fundamental problem because most suggestions would have little effect on existing homeowners, but instead reduce demand from younger generations (or renters). With the overall supply of housing fixed, measures to improve affordability need to have precisely the opposite incidence.

This leads to the second kind of demand-side intervention: policies to increase demand. As with policies to dampen demand, whether this helps in terms of affordability depends on the extent to which it redistributes the ability to demand housing from the house 'rich' to the house 'poor'.

Once again, many recommendations are likely to work in the wrong direction. For example, the Smith Institute has suggested that the Government should consider tax concessions along the lines of mortgage interest tax relief (Miras, which was abolished for principal residences in 2000) to encourage access to home ownership.

Unfortunately, US evidence suggests that there is only a very weak link between mortgage interest relief and home ownership (Hilber and Turner, 2010). In fact, in tightly regulated housing markets, relief has a negative effect on home ownership because the price effect (through increased demand) more than offsets the income effect (from the tax deduction). In less regulated markets, relief does have a positive effect on home ownership rates, but only for higher income groups.

As the UK market is very highly regulated, these findings suggest considerable caution in using Miras as a means to increase home ownership. Reintroducing it could prove to be a costly and ineffective intervention, which has the opposite impact of that intended.

Unfortunately, many other demand-side proposals do not stand up to even the most basic scrutiny. The most recent example is Nick Clegg's suggestion that parents should be allowed to use their pension to help younger people buy property. A two-step assessment of this policy (which can, of course, be applied to many other housing policy initiatives) would run as follows.

First, how many people are likely to be affected? This can be tricky to work out precisely, but for Clegg's announcement – as with a number of recent schemes – the conclusion from a rough estimate seems to be 'not many'. Second, if the policy does affect relatively large numbers of people, what will be the likely impact on the market?

This second step involves applying some basic insights from supply and demand. There are essentially two ways to help people struggling to get a toehold in the housing market. One is to increase the supply of (suitable) housing. The other is to redistribute some of the existing housing stock from older people to younger people. Nick Clegg's proposal does neither of these things – so even if it were to 'work', it would not 'help'.

If it is hard to formulate good demand-side measures when the market is left to its own devices, then another possibility is to intervene directly to redistribute housing. Two popular examples here relate to 'empty bedrooms' and 'empty houses'.

The Intergenerational Foundation has called for the Government to adopt measures to stop older people from 'hoarding' housing. Based on an assessment of housing 'need', policies like this argue that we should take bedrooms from people who currently 'under-occupy' their houses and give them to those who live in overcrowded conditions. In practice, this tends to mean getting old people to move out of large houses.

Ironically, the fact that planning decisions are made on the basis of 'need' but housing is allocated through the market is one of the reasons why the housing market is in such a mess. Markets seek to balance supply and demand (rather than need) and it turns out that as societies get richer, they unsurprisingly tend to demand more space not less.

One response would be to switch to a 'needs'-based mechanism for allocating housing. My colleague Paul Cheshire has light-heartedly suggested one option: 'If we are intent on allocating land for each use without regard to price, then logically we need to introduce space rationing. If price does not determine the supply of land, then price must not determine its consumption. Each adult could, for example, have a ration of, say, 40 square metres with dependent children having, say, another 20 square metres each.

We could, if we wanted, even introduce a trading system so young adults or those willing to live in more cramped conditions could sell some of their space ration, perhaps buying back space in later life' (Cheshire, 2009).

The Intergenerational Foundation suggests something that seems less extreme: measures to encourage homeowners to consume less space. These would be of two kinds. The first would strongly penalise people who 'overconsume' space. Such penalties build up from a logic of housing need and are problematic for all the reasons that space rationing would be: who decides how much space is enough?

The second approach would be to remove barriers and distortions that encourage people to over-consume housing. I would have no problems with such measures apart from the fact that they would be highly costly and remarkably ineffective.

Take, for example, the idea of removing stamp duty on people downsizing. At the moment, the huge wealth gain that they would get by moving into a smaller house is insufficient to offset the benefits of staying put. Removing stamp duty would change this balance for a small number of people at the margin, but it would be at a huge cost to the public finances.

Removing single person allowances on council tax or removing universal benefits for those in valuable houses would have a similarly small impact on the number of people willing to downsize. But it would impose high costs on a small number of people who are income-poor and who do not want to move for whatever reason.

For more wealthy people, this would essentially be an irrelevance.

Changing the treatment of capital gains tax would provide a disincentive for ownership (which may or may not be a good thing) but it would dampen the incentives to downsize. An annual capital gains tax would constitute a punishment based on arbitrary decisions on how much space is enough.

What about empty homes? In England, there are around 280,000 homes that are empty for more than six months. But for 2011, the data show that only 29,500 of these long-term empty homes were in London, with another 32,500 in the South East. In other words, in high demand areas, very few houses are empty.

Using empty homes will (sometimes) make sense, but it will not do much to solve the UK's housing problem. Just as with empty bedrooms, the reallocation of empty homes does not represent a long-term solution to the housing crisis. So what can be done? The short answer is that we must do things to increase the supply of housing.

Increasing the supply of housing

The under-supply of housing in the UK has been a long-term problem, which the previous Government was unable to tackle effectively. Labour was slow to recognise that something needed to be done about the planning system. Once the problem became clear, top-down regional plans were introduced, which tried to force local authorities to build more housing.

These plans were very unpopular with local authorities in parts of the country that needed more housing and were quickly abolished by the Coalition Government. The new 'national planning framework' intends to replace the topdown system with more 'localism' and a package of financial incentives to encourage development – with a target of 240,000 new homes to be built each year (see Nathan and Overman, 2011).

These reforms should be welcomed for a number of reasons, but the Government may yet regret the immediate abolition of regional plans. Uncertainty creates problems for developers who tend to respond by postponing investment until that uncertainty is resolved. Add to this the effects of the recession and you have two underlying reasons for concerns about the supply of housing.

In addition to these short-term issues, there is the longer-term issue of what the Government will do if its package of financial incentives is insufficient to encourage more development. With the new system yet to bed in, it could be a few years before the government is able to assess whether the system is working. The assessment is likely to be close to an election, when a change of Government could see a change of policy and yet more uncertainty for developers.

Another area with which the previous Government struggled was its insistence on high brownfield targets. There are some problems with these targets, but they remain very popular. This means that there is a danger that the Coalition Government will not be able to resist calls to strengthen constraints on building on greenfield land. The Government has already committed to maintaining green belts, but there are many other categories of 'protected land' where long-term policy remains uncertain.

But truly dealing with the problem of affordability requires a market-led response in the areas of highest demand. This in turn requires the planning system to allow a proper supply response. Addressing long-term affordability is not a matter of short-term stimulus. Instead, it requires a private sector response when the market finally picks up. Developing a planning system that allows that to happen is the real challenge.

In all the debate around the Government's planning reforms, we are in danger of losing sight of the fundamental problem: the current system has failed to deliver enough houses of the kind people want in the places where they want to live. Supposedly 'radical' solutions are either insufficiently important to make much difference (empty homes) or so radical that it is hard to believe they represent a good solution (empty bedrooms). The real solution is straightforward: build more housing.

Henry Overman is director of the Spatial Economics Research Centre (SERC), professor of economic geography at LSE and a research associate in CEP's globalisation programme.

For more commentary on housing and other urban and regional policy issues, see the SERC blog: http://spatial-economics.blogspot.co.uk/.

Winter 2012

⇨ The above information originally appeared as 'The UK's Housing Crisis', by Henry G. Overman, in *CentrePiece* Volume 17, Issue 3, Winter 2012 (http://cep.lse.ac.uk/pubs/download/cp382.pdf). Published by the Centre for Economic Performance, London School of Economics and Political Science (http://cep.lse.ac.uk/), December 2012.

Shortage of homes over next 20 years threatens deepening housing crisis

Britain is heading for a property shortage of more than a million homes by 2022 unless the current rate of housebuilding is dramatically increased, according to reports from the Joseph Rowntree Foundation (JRF). The evidence, being presented at the Foundation's Centenary Housing Conference in London, reveals that the supply of housing is already falling behind demand faster than previously recognised.

As well as launching *Land for Housing*, the report from a JRF Inquiry, the conference is debating Britain's housing in 2022, the first in a series of working papers examining the long-term measures needed to tackle social disadvantage. Both warn that the impending housing crisis will hit hardest in London and the South. Although these regions contribute 70 per cent of the rising demand for new homes, only 50 per cent of new homes are currently being built there. By contrast, in the Midlands and the North, there are growing problems of low demand in some areas, and of empty and abandoned property.

The reports highlight the challenges to ministers, planners, housebuilders and housing associations that arise from the pressing need to tackle housing shortages in the South and to achieve an 'urban renaissance' in the Midlands and North. They warn that unless concerted action is taken, areas of high demand for housing will see increased homelessness and a crisis in public services as more nurses, teachers and other staff are priced out of the housing market. The low-demand areas of the North will, meanwhile, experience continuing decline and 'urban exodus'.

Lord Best, Director of the Joseph Rowntree Foundation and author of the working paper, said: 'We estimate that the difference between housing demand and supply will have widened into a yawning gap of 1.1 million homes in England alone by 2022: most of it in London and the South East. This genuinely shocking statistic shows why the time has come for policy makers to recognise that a plentiful supply of new and affordable homes is of the greatest importance to the nation's future health and prosperity.'

He added: 'The bulk of the new homes could go on recycled "brownfield", but this will only happen if there is positive planning, land assembly and decontamination of polluted sites. Investment in our older areas is vital on environmental as well as social and economic grounds. Even so, we have got to be honest and accept that not all of the necessary housing can be built on recycled land. Even if the Government's target of building 60 per cent of new homes on "brownfield" land were met, at least 84,000 homes would need to be built each year on undeveloped "greenfield" sites.'

The opening session of the conference is being introduced and chaired by HRH The Duke of Edinburgh. The event commemorates 100 years since Joseph Rowntree acquired land and started building his 'garden village' of New Earswick outside York. It also marks a decade since the Duke of Edinburgh's Inquiry into British Housing published its final report.

'Housing shortages are set to become one of the most significant social issues of the next 20 years'

The two reports being launched draw on new estimates of the number of extra homes needed in the next 20 years. These are based on population projections published by the Government Actuary's Department at the end of last year and include revised figures on net inward migration to the UK – which is estimated at 135,000 people (43,000 households) a year, compared with 95,000 (30,000 households) a year previously anticipated.

Demand for extra homes in England is now estimated at around 210,000 properties a year, compared with average output from housebuilders and social housing providers of 154,000 extra homes a year over the past five years. The accumulating gap between demand and output points to a shortfall of 1.1 million homes in 20 years' time.

Pressure on the South

Although all regions are expected to see growth in the number of households, the reports note that the greatest pressure will continue to be felt in Southern England. Population changes resulting from internal migration from North to South will be relatively small compared with migration out of London placing added demands

on housing in the rest of the South East. However, natural growth in the population and the level of international migration into London will mean continuing pressure on the capital's housing supply.

The reports stress that the effects of housing shortages in the South fall most heavily on the poorest families who cannot afford to buy and have no access to the oversubscribed rented accommodation provided by local authorities and housing associations. Recent figures show a sharp rise since 1996 in the number of homeless households housed by local authorities in temporary accommodation.

The working paper highlights a long-term decline since 1980 in the provision of subsidised, social housing and insists there can be no substitute for greater public investment in achieving a revival. It points out that both the subsidies to housing providers (such as Social Housing Grant to housing associations) and to individuals (such as Housing Benefit and Income Support for mortgage interest payments) have diminished in recent years.

Land supply

The Land Inquiry report identifies an increased need for 'intermediate' housing markets in areas where property prices are high, to provide homes for lower and middle-income staff. It argues that schemes could be supported by land pooling arrangements similar to those operating in France and Germany, where landowners have incentives to make land collectively available for housing. Another innovation that could help to protect the value of land and ensure its availability when needed for social housing would be the introduction of Community Land Trusts that are widely used in the United States.

The working paper, in addition, emphasises the scope for institutional investment in the private rented sector to generate new homes at market rents, particularly for single people.

Urban extensions

Both reports urge better use of innovations in housing design that make it possible to build attractively at higher densities. The working paper argues that the most effective way for planners to meet the concentration of housing demand in the South is through extensions to existing towns and cities, rather than new towns.

'The greatest pressure will continue to be felt in Southern England'

'Urban extensions' can plug into existing public transport routes, schools, shops and facilities – helping to minimise additional congestion and pollution. By building on a significant scale – with several hundred homes – it is also possible to negotiate greater 'planning gains' with landowners and developers to fund more affordable housing and community amenities.

'Demand for extra homes in England is now estimated at around 210,000 properties a year'

Lord Best said: 'In our view, housing shortages are set to become one of the most significant social issues of the next 20 years. Unless we act now, shortages will lead to overcrowding and homelessness. But they will also have knock-on effects for the whole of society, driving up house prices in areas of high demand, inhibiting economic growth and making it harder for good quality public services to be delivered.'

⇨ The above information is reprinted with kind permission from the Joseph Rowntree Foundation. Please visit www.jrf.org.uk for further information.

© Joseph Rowntree Foundation 2013

The housing crisis and me

Hear from people who are struggling to find housing to meet their needs and have joined the Yes to Homes campaign at www. yestohomes.co.uk.

Amy, 24, Daventry

'Me and my partner separated at the beginning of the year. As a result, me and our two children, aged four and 18 months, moved in with my mum. The following day I went to my local council and explained the whole situation and was told there was nothing they could do as I was the one that left the family home and therefore made myself effectively homeless.

'To get into a private landlord property the upfront fees were £1000 minimum for a one bedroom flat. These people are meant to be here to help!'

Lisa, 28, County Durham

'Me and my partner are a young family with four children – three are girls, and our eldest daughter is at the age where she needs to have her own room due to her growing up.

'We used to live in Newcastle in a private rented house, where the landlord never did any repairs. We lived there for nine years, until last year when our gas boiler and gas meter were both condemned. We tried everything for the housing associations and local authorities to help and after eight weeks of no gas or hot water we had to move away from our friends and family. The stress has nearly destroyed our marriage and we are living too far from our family and friends, who I need around us as my husband is epileptic.

'We just can't settle where we are and now we are finding that a three bedroom isn't big enough but there aren't enough four bedroom houses. Private landlords charge too much for a deposit, especially when you're on a low income. Even if me and my partner worked we would never afford to rent or buy. The way things are going I feel like I have been shoved out of my home town.'

Ceecee, 27, London

'I live in a one bedroom ground floor flat with my two boys who are aged three and eight. When I went to the council to ask how long it could take for me to move, they told me to turn my living room into a bedroom, just keep on bidding, look for home exchange or go private. I don't know what to do because I've been doing everything and three years later I'm still here.'

Judy, 54, London

'I have been temping for a long time and rented privately, but while claiming housing benefit I became behind in my rent and as a result of this have had to move. Private landlords will not give me a tenancy as they say I am not earning enough, and the local council told me they have no duty of care to provide me with housing. So I am staying in a room at a friend's house but I have to move out soon.'

Wayne, 30, Wolverhampton

'We are a family of four – two adults and two children (aged 16 months and four and a half years) – living in a one bedroom third floor flat. After getting this accommodation five years ago, we went straight back on the council waiting list and to this day we have still got nowhere bigger – after no end of phone calls to the council with the promise of a call back, which still to this day has not happened.

'We have had two councillors involved in this, both Labour and Liberal Democrat – again another waste of time. Now I believe this is affecting my partner's and children's health. My eldest is having to have speech therapy and my partner is under a psychologist. I just hope this situation resolves soon before permanent damage is done.'

Mark, 48, Daventry

'I have been separated from my wife for six years. I have a one bedroom flat, and at the weekends and some other times my daughter has to share my bedroom and sleep on the floor. I would like to know my rights as I know this is not acceptable by today's understanding of the law.'

Amanda, 35

'In December 2009 my husband kicked myself and our four children out of our home. We moved in with my mum, and I have put my name on the council waiting list for a house. But I'm still having to share a

> That's a small bedroom.
>
> That used to be a closet.

bedroom with four children all boys aged six, five, two and one years old. I feel like the council are doing nothing to help.'

Alice, 34, London

'I am a single mother of two young children under the age of ten. I receive no maintenance money from the father, despite going through the CSA, and am struggling to find accommodation for myself and my family. I had to leave the marital home five years ago due to a violent relationship, and had no choice but to move into my mother's house to escape. I have been here for five years now.

'I am unable to go onto the housing register due to having a small lump sum of money from my ex-husband buying me out of our old flat as part of our divorce. But this money is not enough to get me onto the housing ladder on my own. Even though I work full time, the largest mortgage I can get is £108,000 which with my savings would mean under £150,000 for a flat in London – this is not possible. Shared ownership sounds like a good idea but I have found that you have to either live or work in the area of the development to even stand a chance of getting a flat. There seems to be very few, if any, in Haringey? So what are my options? Renting? Well earning £1,300 a month and a one bed flat in Haringey being at the very least £900 per month – I simply can't afford it. It would be pointless going to work.

'Where is the sense in cutting the housing budget when there are people like me and many more far worse off? What options do we have? I certainly do not know where I am going to go in three months time when I have to leave my mother's, as the house is in disrepair. On the street?

Gail, 42, Rochdale

'I live with my two teenage children in a three bed house. I met my husband to be and he was going to move into my house. Six weeks before our wedding, social services took his three children from his ex-wife, and we took them in. My house was too small, so he got put in a flat until they got him a house.

'After one year of being married we live three miles apart from each other with no sign of a house together. All of the big council houses are full and under-occupied. We both work, but don't earn enough to buy a five bed house that we need. Our MP has been a help writing letters, and social services are also helping.'

Salima, 49

'I am a single mother, and I live with my two children aged 14 and 18. Both of my children are in full time education. Although I hold a British passport and both my children were born in the UK, we have nobody to rely on and our private rent contract expires in June.'

Alison, 37

'My partner bought a three bedroom house for us, but our relationship broke down three months later. I have a nine-month-old baby with him, and a 13-year-old from a previous relationship. I went to the council but they said I wasn't in need of a house as I have one and my ex-partner has to provide a house for his daughter and my other daughter as he bought the property as a family home.

'I have been trying to get a private let with the home bond as a deposit and then I can get housing benefit, but no one will take the home bond as a deposit – they want one month's deposit and one month's rent cash.'

Estera, 28

'I have a ten-month old daughter, and in January I became a single mum. I am renting a flat, and pay £680 rent every month, but my wages are only £206 every week. I have applied for housing benefit, but have to wait another five weeks for a decision. I feel devastated and worry so much about my daughter – how can I give her what she needs?'

Sarah, 33, Portsmouth

'I live in a two bedroom flat on the eighth floor of a tower block with my two children. My son is ten and my daughter will be seven in May. Both my children have disabilities, and my daughter uses a disabled buggy.

'I applied to move while pregnant with my daughter. I got in touch with my councillor, and a year before my son

was ten I was visited my a member of my council who saw the cramped state I lived in and moved me up to fourth on the list and told me I could only be waiting for up to four months.

'A year later I am still waiting. I'm not down in the higher priority list, which is full, but in the medium priority list. I am still number four, and the person who is top has been their since 2008. Unless you go private and find somewhere who takes housing benefit you are stuck.'

Laura, 39, London

'We are a family of five comprising of our two daughters aged six years and six weeks, our four-year-old son, my husband and myself.

'We live in Stratford, London in a one bedroom flat on the second floor. For the past four years we have been in contact with our housing officers, local MP and even the Mayor for Newham in regards to our overcrowded situation.

'As you can imagine the situation has become desperate after the birth of our third child six weeks ago.

'I have exhausted nearly every option to be re-housed, and the situation is getting desperate. Where do we, a young family who want the best start for our family, go when it seems that we get stonewalled at every turn?'

⇨ The above information is reprinted with kind permission from the National Housing Federation. Please visit www. housing.org.uk for further information.

© National Housing Federation 2013

Building more homes

Shelter believes the solution to England's housing crisis lies in building more homes. The Government has said that building more homes is a priority and Shelter is campaigning to ensure that the right actions are taken to build the homes we need.

Successive governments have failed to get on top of our housing crisis. Years of insufficient investment in building new homes has left many people unable to buy or rent the homes they need to get on in life. The Government needs to continue thinking innovatively to make sure that this generation and the next aren't denied a stable and affordable home.

Why more homes are needed

Supply of new homes is failing to keep pace with demand

England is currently suffering from a huge housing shortage, especially in terms of affordable homes. This shortage is due to the fact that low rates of house building over several decades have failed to keep up with increasing demand, as the number of households increases. Large amounts of social housing stock have also been sold off under the Right to Buy scheme and not replaced.

The current crisis

With new housing supply failing to keep pace with demand, housing costs have risen rapidly, sparking an affordability crisis. Large numbers of people have found themselves priced out of buying or even renting a home. This problem is particularly acute for young people and those on low or average incomes, who are unable to get a foot on the property ladder or afford their rent.

In England:

⇨ More than 75,000 households were found to be homeless by local authorities in 2011/12. [1]

⇨ At the end of June 2012, 51,640 homeless households were living in temporary accommodation in England. [2]

⇨ There are currently more than 400,000 households living in overcrowded conditions. [3]

England's housing situation has reached crisis proportions. We desperately need more homes now.

Delivering the homes people want

It is critical that any new homes built benefit new residents and existing communities alike. This means building the right kind of homes, in the right places, with the right infrastructure. At present, there is a shortage of decent, family-sized accommodation, but England needs more homes in all sizes – for sale, for rent and for intermediate tenures like shared ownership.

Shelter understands that new homes must be desirable places to live. We want to avoid repeating mistakes of the 1960s and 1970s where the quality of housing developments was sometimes sacrificed in a drive to build homes quickly. New developments must include the necessary supporting infrastructure and services to create thriving communities. They should be well-designed, attractive, spacious and efficient to heat and maintain.

Campaign demands

We want national and local government to prioritise building more homes and to work with housing associations, private developers and investors and communities to ensure that priority becomes action. The Government should adopt the following measures:

⇨ Increase capital investment in new affordable housing provision and infrastructure

⇨ Provide investment guarantees to housing associations

⇨ Make effective use of public land to support affordable housebuilding

⇨ Use all money raised from Right to Buy sales to invest in new homes locally

⇨ Use levies raised from changes to stamp duty and capital gains tax to help ordinary families get a home

⇨ Make it easier for local councils to build homes

⇨ Make it easier for alternative methods of housebuilding, such as Community Land Trusts and self-build, to make a real contribution

⇨ Ensure that a decent proportion of new homes are suitable for families, for older people and for other specific groups.

[1] Statutory Homelessness Statistics, Communities and Local Government 2012.

[2] Statutory Homelessness Statistics, Communities and Local Government, 2012.

[3] English Housing Survey 2010/11, Communities and Local Government, 2012.

⇨ The above information is reprinted with kind permission from Shelter. Please visit www.shelter.org.uk for further information.

© Shelter 2013

Plans to boost UK house building, jobs and the economy

PM: 'This Government is serious about rolling its sleeves up and doing all it can to kick-start the economy.'

The Prime Minister and Deputy Prime Minister have announced a major housing and planning package that will help deliver:

⇨ Up to 70,000 new homes, including affordable housing and opportunities for first-time buyers to get onto the housing ladder

⇨ 140,000 jobs and a boost to the construction sector

⇨ A £40 billion guarantee for major infrastructure projects and £10 billion for new homes.

This includes a series of measures aimed at supporting businesses, developers and first-time buyers, while slashing unnecessary red tape across the planning system.

The measures include:

⇨ Removing restrictions on house builders to help unlock 75,000 homes currently stalled due to sites being commercially unviable. Developers who can prove that council's costly affordable housing requirements make the project unviable will see them removed.

⇨ New legislation for government guarantees of up to £40 billion worth of major infrastructure projects and up to £10 billion of new homes. The Infrastructure (Financial Assistance) Bill will include guaranteeing the debt of Housing Associations and private sector developers.

⇨ Up to 15,000 affordable homes and bring 5,000 empty homes back into use using new capital funding of £300 million and the infrastructure guarantee.

⇨ An additional 5,000 homes built for rent at market rates in line with proposals outlined in Sir Adrian Montague's report to the Government on boosting the private rented sector.

⇨ Thousands of big commercial and residential applications to be directed to a major infrastructure fast track, and where councils are poor developers can opt to have their decision taken by the Planning Inspectorate.

⇨ Calling time on poor performing town hall planning departments, putting the worst into 'special measures' if they have failed to improve the speed and quality of their work and allowing developers to bypass councils. More applications also will go into a fast track appeal process.

⇨ 16,500 first-time buyers helped with a £280 million extension of the successful 'FirstBuy' scheme, which offers aspiring homeowners a much-needed deposit and a crucial first step on the housing ladder.

⇨ For a time-limited period, slashing planning red tape, including sweeping away the rules and bureaucracy that prevent families and businesses from making improvements to their properties, helping tens of thousands of homeowners and companies.

'This Government is serious about rolling its sleeves up and doing all it can to kick-start the economy'

The Prime Minister said:

'The measures announced today show this Government is serious about rolling its sleeves up and doing all it can to kick-start the economy. Some of the proposals are controversial; others have been a long time in coming. But along with our Housing Strategy, they provide a comprehensive plan to unleash one of the biggest home-building programmes this country has seen in a generation. That means more investment around the county; more jobs for our people; and more young families able to realise their dreams and get on the housing ladder.'

The Deputy Prime Minister said:

'This is a Coalition Government, determined to get on with the job of delivering a healthier economy. Today's major boost to housing and planning will make it easier to build a home, easier to buy a first home and easier to extend a home. A boost that will get Britain building again. Building thousands of affordable homes and generating thousands of new jobs.'

6 September 2012

⇨ The above information is reprinted with kind permission from GOV.UK. Please visit www.gov.uk for further information.

© Crown copyright 2013

'Travelodge families': the new face of the housing crisis

Benefit changes, rising private rents, and depleted social housing all force councils to spend billions at Travelodge and Premier Inn in stop-gap measures to help evicted families.

By Oliver Wright

Budget hotel chains are being paid thousands of pounds a year to accommodate the homeless as local councils attempt to tackle Britain's growing housing crisis.

The percentage of homeless families in hotels or bed and breakfast accommodation is now at its highest level for a decade, government figures show. And, as a result, spending by Britain's largest cities on so-called 'bed and breakfast accommodation' has increased by 25 percent the past year to £91.1 million.

Part of the rise is fuelled by councils having to place people in budget hotel chains such as Travelodge while they seek a more permanent solution.

The situation is particularly acute in Oxford, Cambridge and London, where rent rises in the private sector have outstripped the budgets that councils have set aside to pay for emergency accommodation. Other areas where councils have been forced to adopt this costly stop-gap include Edinburgh, Huntingdon, Herts, north Devon and Chorley, Lancashire.

A number of councils have now concluded that chains such a Travelodge and Premier Inn offer better value than the smaller hostels which have traditionally been used.

Ed Turner, the Deputy Leader of Oxford City Council, said the situation was 'grim' and added: 'The reason we use places like Travelodge is because you can't find anywhere else.

'I've spoken to a parent who has had to move his children to a Travelodge because he was being evicted from the home he had occupied – and he had no idea how he was going to get his kids to school. Think of the consequence for a family with kids in school – yes, it's a problem for our finances but, much more importantly, it's a problem for those affected.'

Mr Turner said that the problem facing cities such as Oxford was two-fold. On one hand, rental property prices were rising at a faster rate that housing benefit – that has been capped by the Government – meaning many private landlords are giving notice to social tenants who cannot find alternative accommodation, forcing them into homelessness.

At the same time councils are finding it increasingly hard to maintain their stock of emergency housing to put families up who have been made homeless.

'If you put the local housing benefits allowance rate for Oxford into the RightMove website only two properties come up in the entire city which are affordable,' he said.

'Placing people in somewhere like a Travelodge is a last resort but sometimes it has to be done to meet the council's legal and, frankly, moral obligations.'

A spokesman for Huntingdon District Council said it had also had to use Premier Inns to meet a shortfall in accommodation for the homeless.

'We do have houses that we rent for emergency accommodation

in the private sector but we are struggling to recruit new landlords because they can get higher rents elsewhere,' he said.

David Greening, the Housing Advice Service manager at Cambridge City Council agreed that the situation was 'not ideal for families at all'.

'Stays in any form of temporary accommodation are unsettling for people,' he said.

The Conservative-run Borough Council of Wellingborough in Northants spent £1,961 in a single week to house a family while Liberal Democrat-controlled Eastleigh, in Hampshire, spent £1,932 to accommodate a family with seven children for a seven-day stay. Labour's North East Derbyshire district council spent almost £700 for a week, while Dartford said it had a bill of £616 for one week for a family of five.

Recent figures uncovered by the Labour Party showed that the use of B&Bs to house homeless families beyond six weeks had risen by 800 per cent since 2010 – a huge cost to the councils concerned.

And over the past four years, according to research by the Bureau of Investigative Journalism, the UK has spent almost £2 billion in temporary housing for homeless families – enough to build 72,000 homes.

Shadow housing minister Jack Dromey said the use of budget hotels was a 'clear sign' that the coalition Government's housing policies were failing. 'It's a disgrace,' he said. 'It might be good business for hotel chains but it's bad value for the taxpayer and completely inappropriate for homeless families who have no place else to go.

'Rather than asking if there's room at the inn, the Government should be building the homes the country desperately needs.'

A Travelodge spokesperson said: 'Local councils around the UK sometimes use our hotels, to provide temporary accommodation for individuals and families who are made homeless due to an emergency incident such as flooding or a fire. The Council book the hotels directly via our website like any other business and leisure customer. We have over 500 hotels across the country and providing good value accommodation is our day to day business.'

A Premier Inn spokesman said: 'On an occasional basis Premier Inn is asked by some local councils to provide accommodation for residents who may temporarily not be able to live in their home address.'

Housing Minister Mark Prisk said: 'The law is clear that families should only be placed in this temporary accommodation in an emergency and only then for no more than six weeks. It is also a waste of tax payers' money to be paying such large sums to house families in this way.

'Whilst it is ultimately a matter for councils to decide how to make best use of their budgets,

it cannot make sense to pay more for housing a family in one room than it would cost to house them in suitable self-contained accommodation.'

A Travelodge spokesperson said: 'Local councils around the UK sometimes use our hotels, to provide temporary accommodation for individuals and families who are made homeless due to an emergency incident such as flooding or a fire. The Council book the hotels directly via our website like any other business and leisure customer. We have over 500 hotels across the country and providing good value accommodation is our day to day business.'

Case study: There were five of us in one small hotel room

Agnieszka Bartczak, her partner Piotr Debacz, and her three small children, aged two, three and five became homeless last winter after being evicted from their home in Cambridgeshire.

They appealed to Huntingdonshire District Council for help, which, restricted by a shortage of suitable accommodation, put them up in a Premier Inn by the busy A1.

The measure was supposed to be temporary while more suitable housing was arranged, but seven weeks later the family continued to live in one small room.

Speaking to her local paper at the time, 22-year-old Agnieszka said: 'They told us we need to find somewhere to stay the night and we have been here ever since.

'There are five people in one room and there just isn't enough space. We are in desperate need of somewhere else to stay.'

28 May 2013

⇨ The above information is reprinted with kind permission from *The Independent*. Please visit www.independent.co.uk for further information.

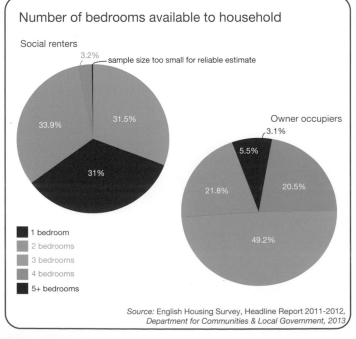

Number of bedrooms available to household

Social renters

3.2% — sample size too small for reliable estimate

33.9%

31.5%

31%

Owner occupiers

3.1%

5.5%

21.8%

20.5%

49.2%

- 1 bedroom
- 2 bedrooms
- 3 bedrooms
- 4 bedrooms
- 5+ bedrooms

Source: English Housing Survey, Headline Report 2011-2012, Department for Communities & Local Government, 2013

Councils plan to build 270,000 fewer homes

Councils across England have radically reduced their housing targets. This has contributed to a situation where the Coalition could end up presiding over the lowest level of housebuilding.

New research from Policy Exchange shows that councils are planning to build 272,720 fewer new homes since the abolition of regional planning. The figures, produced by planning consultancy Tetlow King, show that since the revocation of Regional Spatial Strategies in 2010, local authorities have used their beefed up planning powers to reduce housing targets. The largest reductions are in the South East (-57,049) and South West (-108,380), areas with the greatest housing shortage.

The report says lowering housing targets will eventually lead to fewer homes being built. Although the targets are seldom hit, they govern the release of land for housing, meaning less land will be made available. Without significant changes to the planning system, housing numbers will continue to fall over time.

The report argues that the Government should not be too aggressive toward councils reducing targets, except where they are clearly ignoring their responsibilities. It argues that instead the Government should focus on ensuring councils actually deliver the homes their targets propose.

It proposes:

⇨ increasing the power and number of neighbourhood plans and directly channelling funds from the Community Infrastructure Levy to households affected by new development

⇨ converting more brownfield sites into housing

Alex Morton, author of the report, 'The Prime Minister and the Deputy Prime Minister have rightly made it clear that we need to build more homes. Yet the Government is on track to preside over the lowest level of housebuilding since the 1920s.

'Relying on councils to expand housing targets was a mistake. However, now the Coalition should focus on fixing the multiple failures with the housing market – not fighting councils. This can help us begin to build the homes we need.'

28 December 2012

⇨ The above information is reprinted with kind permission from Policy Exchange. Please visit www.policy exchange.org.uk for further information.

© Policy Exchange 2013

Concerns over planning reforms

54% of the British public concerned that removing planning permission will worsen the quality of their neighbourhood.

Over half (54%) of the British public believe that the Government's plans to remove the need for planning permission for house and building extensions would mean the quality of the design of their neighbourhood would get worse, according to a YouGov poll commissioned by the Royal Institute of British Architects (RIBA).

⇨ 54% of respondents think the quality of the design of buildings and houses in their neighbourhood would get worse.

⇨ 25% say it would remain the same.

⇨ Only 7% think that it will get better.

Losing influence

In addition to concerns over design quality, the poll also revealed that half of respondents are worried that under the Government's proposed planning reforms they would lose their influence over new extensions in their local area.

⇨ 31% said they were 'fairly worried' about losing influence under the new regime, while 20% of respondents said they were 'very worried'.

⇨ 30% said they were 'not very worried' about losing influence, and 10% were not worried at all.

Commenting on the poll results, RIBA Past President and Chair of the RIBA Planning Group, Ruth Reed said: 'We agree that there is a need to reduce the red tape in our current planning system but as the British public have clearly expressed, this policy change must be more carefully considered to ensure we make our neighbourhoods better not worse.'

21 September 2012

⇨ The above information is reprinted with kind permission from YouGov. Please visit www.yougov.co.uk for further information.

© YouGov 2013

Affordable housing target 'on track'

Press release from the Rural Services Network, November 2012.

The Government's housing agency is expected to meet targets to build more affordable homes.

The Homes and Communities Agency said it was on track to meet its delivery targets for 2012/13, following official statistics published on Friday (16 November 2012).

In the first six months of the year, the agency completed 11,981 homes and started on site with a further 5,243, according to the statistics.

'Developers typically complete more homes during in the second half of an average year'

Of the homes completed, 6,375 were affordable – with a further 3,499 delivered under FirstBuy – equating to 38% of the agency's annual targets for affordable housing and FirstBuy combined.

Developers typically complete more homes during the second half of an average year, prompting the agency to forecast that it will meet its 2012/13 target.

This goal is a combined affordable housing and FirstBuy corporate plan target of 26,250 completions by the end of March 2013.

Agency chief executive Pat Ritchie said: 'With these half year statistics demonstrating a typical delivery profile, we are on track to meet our targets for the year.'

Of the homes started on site, 3,310 were affordable, of which 96% came through the new Affordable Homes Programme, reflecting the predicted delivery profile.

The agency said it was also on track with its contribution of 123,000 new affordable homes to meet the Government's aspiration to deliver up to 170,000 affordable homes by 2015.

Of these, some 55,000 affordable homes had been completed to date, equating to just under 45% of the delivery for which the agency is responsible.

'The Government's housing agency is expected to meet targets to build more affordable homes'

Ms Ritchie said: 'This is testament to the commitment of our partners and the action we have taken to build momentum in the new AHP.'

She added: 'It's particularly pleasing that FirstBuy is performing so strongly with 3,499 completions, and that of the affordable housing starts virtually all of them came through the AHP.'

Ms Ritchie said it was also pleasing that a total of 55,000 new affordable homes had been completed – nearly half of those the agency was tasked with delivering by 2015.

'FirstBuy is performing so strongly with 3,499 completions'

A detailed breakdown of statistics – which exclude delivery in London – is available to download from the agency's Housing Statistics web page.

16 November 2012

⇨ The above information is reprinted with kind permission from the Rural Services Network. Please visit www.rsnonline.org.uk for further information.

© Rural Services Network Online

Should expensive council properties be sold off to solve our housing problems?

A right-wing think tank has suggested councils should sell off expensive houses to fund new building developments.

Policy Exchange, an influential think tank set up by Conservative MP Nick Boles – an ally of Prime Minister David Cameron – said the UK could afford to build 170,000 affordable homes a year by putting the highest-value properties on the market when they become vacant.

But the think tank has been accused of pushing for the poor to be driven out of wealthy areas, and Labour MP Karen Buck has said the policy doesn't make sense and would break up communities. Read these arguments, and see what you think.

Alex Morton

Head of housing, Policy Exchange.

In England we face both a housing crisis and a growth crisis. Despite high house prices and high and rising rents, the number of homes started last year fell 4% to 98,000. Meanwhile, housing waiting lists are at over 1.8 million households. Individuals and families are trapped waiting in often unsuitable accommodation. As part of trying to get the nation's finances back on track, spend on new homes has been shredded. This is a roll call of doom.

Fortunately we think a policy exists that is very popular, fair, and could boost the number of homes built by between 80,000 and 170,000 a year; nearly double or triple the current total of homes built in the UK. At present, around 20% of the social housing stock in this country is 'expensive'. It is worth more than the average for that size property within the same region (e.g. the North West, London). We believe selling this off as it becomes empty could raise £4.5 billion a year – as much as the last spending round managed over four. 30,000 homes are being sold off annually to fund building many new homes in the same area.

Behind the cold figures, the practical reality of current policy beggars belief. I was born in a council flat. My parents hoped for something free of damp in inner city Birmingham. They certainly didn't expect a large and expensive townhouse. This policy isn't just unfair to the taxpayer but also the nearly two million families and individuals on the social housing waiting list. One single family gets a house that most taxpayers can't afford (unfair) and force others to wait for possibly years (unfair). The public agree. 73% believe that social tenants should not be offered new properties worth more than the average in the local authority. 60% agreed that social tenants should not be offered new properties in expensive an area. Even social tenants agree with changing the current system.

Some argue that changing current policy will create ghettos and cause mass unemployment. This is simply wrong. Even over time we are only selling 20% of the social housing stock. So most social houses aren't affected. This policy would mix social stock in the bottom 50% of homes and give a 2:1 private: social split, so it doesn't isolate social tenants. What we should be aiming for is decent quality homes as we built in the 1930s or late 1940s. There should be a minimum value as well as a maximum value. Homes and space and gardens achieved via local control over the design and quality of what is built. It is pretty insulting and patronising to say anywhere outside the top half of properties is a 'ghetto'.

On employment, there is a weak link between employment in an area and the value of its housing. Even assuming that the link is 100% causal (living in a more expensive area raises your chance of a job, not just people with jobs live in more expensive areas), the cost per job is £2.5 million. This eye-watering sum compares to £33,000 per job the Regional Growth Fund creates – it is 56 times more expensive. Because of commuting location within an area isn't that key for jobs. But while we're on employment, this policy creates 340,000 jobs – a desperately needed shot in the arm for the economy and also many unskilled jobs – which we urgently need.

Existing tenants are not affected by this measure. We need to get a grip on housing policy. This is a quick and popular option to help get the economy going and people housed. Government cannot afford to delay.

Alex Morton is head of housing at Policy Exchange.

Karen Buck

Labour Member of Parliament for Westminster North and Shadow Education Minister.

The suggestion by the Policy Exchange think-tank that social housing in valuable areas should be sold and the profits used to build more homes in cheaper places, re-hashes an old argument but predictably grabbed the headlines.

Doesn't it make sense, with 4.5 million people in housing need, to boost supply? Surely those in need and on low incomes should not expect to be housed centrally anyway (the myth-makers like to refer to 'Mayfair' or 'near Harrods' as if these neighbourhoods of the global mega-rich are stuffed with council estates).

Well, no, it doesn't make sense. Because behind the beguiling simplicity of the idea lie some complex realities, and as an MP for North Westminster, and previously for the much-cited example of Notting Hill, I have some knowledge of these.

Let's start with the fact that social housing has existed in inner London for 150 years, since the big social philanthropists like the Peabody Trust started replacing the slums which had long existed alongside Parliament, Covent Garden, etc.

Swathes of what now include some of the country's most expensive properties were once desperately poor. Even as recently as the 1960s, the Notting Hill Housing Trust started by buying and replacing private homes that were a by-word for slum landlordism – somewhat ironically paving the way for the regeneration which now sees houses there sell for many millions. London has always

been socially mixed, is now highly ethnically mixed, and has benefited economically, culturally and socially as a result – and social housing has helped make that possible.

Yet more recently still, certainly in Central London, the international property market has surrounded many poorer neighbourhoods, leaving them like islands in a sea of fantastic wealth. It is now estimated that 60% of new sales in central London go to overseas buyers and £5 billion a year is flowing into 'luxury' housing, feeding the house price bubble and freezing out low- and middle-income buyers and renters. Is the answer to surrender to the tide and let it sweep all before it?

Sales are the only way to deal with the shortfall anyway. Notting Hill Housing Trust originally bought properties to protect poor people locally, but as these grew massively in value the balance sheet of the organisation strengthened and became the foundation for hundreds of millions of pounds of prudential borrowing for more social homes elsewhere. The same applies to all the other social landlords who operate in 'rich' areas. It wasn't necessary to sell the homes to use their value to create more homes elsewhere, as they proved. New investment made sense in itself, as well, which is why the previous Government had an £8 billion investment programme which the Conservatives slashed by 60%. That programme passed the value test – creating an asset that will make a profit in its lifetime, and pay off in jobs created and benefit bills reduced, but it was decimated.

The number of council homes has already plummeted over the last 30 years because of Right to Buy with boroughs like my own seeing a near-halving of stock. When this policy came in, Margaret Thatcher promised lots of new homes from the proceeds, but the sold homes were never replaced and most of the money disappeared into the Treasury. Some ex-council homes were rented back to low-income and homeless households at much higher prices – helping fuel the rise

in Housing Benefit. People who would once have been eligible for a council home ended up in expensive private rented homes, with the same effect. So the promise was made and broken before. Would it be different now?

Finally, let's return to the issue of 'mixed communities'. We hear a great deal about promoting mixed communities in poor places, like the East End boroughs of Newham, or the south London borough of Southwark. Quite right too – everyone understands that concentrating poorer people in poor neighbourhoods is bad for their life chances and for communities – we were debating this last August when the riots took hold. Those councils want a mix, with more homeownership and greater affluence. So we can't put more council homes there, then. Yet those arguing for mixed communities in that instance don't apply the same logic where low-cost housing is currently limited, because those areas have become more valuable, or because they are away from the inner city, in suburbs, towns and even villages elsewhere. Will London's outer suburbs, or market towns in the surrounding countryside build hundreds of thousands of new council homes and, crucially, offer them to those people, outsiders by definition, squeezed from the inner city?

Or, as seems likely, will already affluent areas become ever more so, communities be broken up and the millions in housing need become more marginalised still?

Karen Buck is the Labour Member of Parliament for Westminster North and Shadow Education Minister.

⇨ The above information is reprinted with kind permission from *The Huffington Post (UK)*. Please visit www. huffingtonpost.co.uk for further information.

Bringing back terraced streets could solve housing crisis, says think tank

Rebuilding traditional streets of terraced housing could cut crime and raise living standards while still housing more people than high-rise blocks, a report has concluded.

By John Bingham, Social Affairs Editor

Policy Exchange, the influential conservative thinktank, is calling for an ambitious bulldozing programme to rid city skylines of thousands of ageing tower blocks and bring back traditional street patterns.

It calculates that, if properly planned, such a scheme could create hundreds of thousands of new homes in addition to those being replaced.

The plan is also likely to reduce crime and anti-social behaviour and improve standards of health and even educational attainment, it argues.

In a report published today, the thinktank sets out plans to transform inner city London, creating homes for more than a million people, but which could be replicated across the country.

By selling off extra housing built, the system could even pay for itself while spelling an end to high-rise tower blocks and 'no-go zone' estates, it is claimed.

The report dismisses as a 'myth' the idea that high-rise estates were built to accommodate growing populations after the Second World War.

It shows that most such estates in the UK are less densely populated than traditional terraces because of the large concrete areas and walkways included as part of the design.

But a mix of traditional two-storey terraces, each with their own front door, and larger houses accommodating flats and maisonettes could almost double the number of homes per hectare currently seen in most inner city areas, the thinktank estimates.

It calculates that 360,000 high-rise flats built between 1950 and 1980 in London alone could be torn down to make way for around 600,000 new houses and flats.

When everyone living in the old properties had been rehoused, there could be about 260,000 new homes available for sale to pay for the projects.

That would be enough to meet the target for building new homes in the capital for the next eight years.

The report, entitled *Create Streets*, points to a string of studies linking high-rise culture with higher crime rates, lower levels of educational attainment and poorer health.

Nicholas Boys Smith, co-author of the report, said: 'It's time we ripped down the mistakes of the past and started building proper streets where people want to live.

'We must not repeat mistakes by building housing which makes people's lives a misery.

'Bulldozing the high-rise tower blocks and no-go zone estates and replacing them with terraced homes and low-rise flats is the best way to build both the number and the quality of homes that we need.'

Last year Policy Exchange prompted controversy with a report calling for councils to sell off their most valuable houses and use the money to build hundreds of thousands of cheaper homes. It won the backing of the Housing Minister Grant Shapps.

24 January 2013

⇨ The above information was reprinted with kind permission from *The Telegraph*. Please visit www.telegraph.co.uk for further information.

© John Bingham/
The Daily Telegraph 2013

'It's a tragedy there's 31,000 empty homes when so many need a place to live' – Peter Black, AM

The Welsh Liberal Democrats will be using their debate this week to call for an empty homes strategy, after a poll was held by the party asking for people to decide what should be debated in the National Assembly.

Marking the first time a political party has ever done such a thing, the Welsh Liberal Democrats launched an online poll in January asking people what they wanted debated in the National Assembly for Wales. A debate calling for a Welsh strategy for bringing empty homes back into use was chosen.

Peter Black, Welsh Lib Dem Shadow Minister for Housing, commented:

'Empty homes are a huge problem here in Wales, as can be seen by the support this issue received in our poll. It's an absolute tragedy that there are over 31,000 empty homes across the whole of Wales just sitting there going to waste while there are so many people on the housing waiting list. Welsh Labour has done too little on this and more must be done to tackle the problem.

'After a decade of near inaction from the Welsh Labour Government, the Welsh Liberal Democrats are using our debate to call on the Welsh Government to develop a strategy that will help local authorities bring empty homes back into use.

'It is essential that we equip our local authorities with more effective tools if we are to make real progress on this issue. This is why the Welsh Liberal Democrats want councils to be allowed flexibility in their approach to council tax.

'The "Houses into Homes" initiative is a welcome start, helped in particular by the fact that the initial £5 million identified for the scheme was doubled to £10 million following the budget deal between the Welsh Liberal Democrats and the Welsh Government last year. But we believe this scheme needs to be developed much further, including ensuring there is more information out there for people to access.'

Kirsty Williams, Leader of the Welsh Liberal Democrats, said:

'We decided to run this poll because we wanted to give people a direct say in what is discussed in the chamber.

'Quality, affordable housing is getting more and more out of reach for the average worker and this problem is even more acute in rural areas, such as in my Brecon and Radnorshire constituency. In rural areas the gap between wages and house prices is often the largest and it is where the development of new affordable housing is often the most challenging due to the particular nature of planning policy in rural areas.

'In Scotland the Government has invested £4.5 million in its Empty Homes Local Fund. Of this total, £2 million is being targeted at renovating empty homes in rural areas in recognition of the particular challenges being faced there. We will be using this debate to call on the Welsh Labour Government to consider whether rural areas in Wales would benefit from similar targeted support.

'This is a hugely important issue that the Welsh Labour Government hasn't done anywhere near enough to tackle. Not only are empty homes a blight on our communities, but they are an immense waste when you consider the high number of people that are in desperate need of a home.'

19 February 2013

⇨ The above information is reprinted with kind permission from the Welsh Liberal Democrats. Please visit www. welshlibdems.org.uk for further information.

Cash to tackle empty homes

New funding could bring more than 400 empty homes back into use for communities across Scotland, Deputy First Minister Nicola Sturgeon said today.

17 housing associations, councils and house builders submitted successful bids for the Scottish Government's Empty Homes Loans Fund.

The fund will help private owners renovate empty homes in exchange for them being made available as affordable housing for at least five years.

There are around 25,000 empty homes across Scotland that are classed as long-term empty located in urban, rural and island communities.

Ms Sturgeon said:

'Empty homes are a blight on many communities across Scotland. Standing empty these properties are no use to anyone. Renovated, they could provide much needed new homes for hundreds of people.

'That is why more needs to be done to make better use of these existing assets.

'Bringing empty homes back into use makes sense because it is a cost-effective way of increasing the supply of housing available to families across Scotland's communities.

'The Empty Homes Loan Fund, and wider work being taken forward by councils as a result of the Shelter Scotland-led Scottish Empty Homes Partnership, can help significantly reduce the number of wasted, empty homes across Scotland.'

Kristen Hubert, coordinator of the Scottish Empty Homes Partnership, which is hosted by Shelter Scotland and funded by the Scottish Government, said:

'It is pleasing and highly encouraging that so many worthy projects have been given the go ahead.

'Having an incentive like a loan to offer owners of empty homes is a key part of getting people to engage with our growing network of Empty Homes Officers and make positive choices about their properties. We will work with the successful bidders to help them make the most of their projects.

'We look forward with excitement to seeing so many empty homes that previously caused issues for their communities coming back to life as affordable housing.'

Councillor Harry McGuigan from COSLA said:

'The fund is a welcome contribution to Scotland's overall housing stock, and will greatly assist local government's empty home officers on making real progress locally in relieving housing pressure.

'Encouraging owners to bring housing stock back to the affordable rental market will make a valuable contribution in tackling homelessness, directly and indirectly, and remove what can be neighbourhood blight.'

27 December 2012

⇨ The above information is reprinted with kind permission from Scotland.gov. Please visit www.scotland.gov.uk for further information.

© Scotland.gov 2013

A right to reclaim abandoned property

Homes for Homes campaign for a right to reclaim...

We believe that the full potential of abandoned property will never be utilised unless people are given the power to use it. We're not advocating squatting, requisitioning, or anything remotely draconian. Indeed, our proposal is one that seeks a fair way of allowing people to use empty property that also meets the interests of the owner. We propose a new legal right empowering communities and citizens, to reclaim abandoned property. This right would be open to all communities and citizens allowing them the right to make a claim to use an empty property as their home.

The right would build on powers set out in 'Community Right to Reclaim Land' and would have the effect of bringing the powers similar to those available to local authorities (Empty Dwelling Management Orders) to communities at large.

This would allow them to make a claim on an empty property setting out how they would make better use of it than the current owner. It would allow their claims to be independently judged against the

owner's proposals, and where their claim was judged to be the best use of the property, provide the community with rights to use the property.

How it would work

Communities and citizens would have the right to make a claim on any residential property that is empty and has been empty for at least two years. Any claim would be made to an independent adjudicating body such as the Residential Property Tribunal. Where the property is publicly owned the adjudicating body would have the power to make an order granting rights to the community to use the property.

The rights of private property owners would be protected. The process would provide an opportunity for communities to negotiate with private owners over the use of empty property, but there would be no order or compulsion for the owner to accept.

Making a claim

The power would be open to all communities and citizens; and could be used for any residential property that had been empty for at least two years.

A claimant would need to make a claim to an independent adjudicating body. To be accepted as a claim a claimant would need to demonstrate the following:

⇨ Evidence of who owns the property

⇨ Evidence that the property has been empty continuously for at least two years

⇨ How the claimant would bring the property into use (including how any costs would be met, and any

proposed alterations to the property itself, and proposed time-scales)

⇨ That the claimant intends to use the property as their sole home, or the community intend to use the property to provide a home for a member of the community.

⇨ Details of payment (if any) the claimant proposes to offer the owner for use of the property

⇨ How long the claimant intends to use the property for.

Processing the claim

The claim would be sent to the property owner with a right to respond. Public owners of property would be required to respond to the claim, setting out their own proposals for the property within a specified time (say 21 days).

Private owners would be invited (but not required) to respond in the same way.

The adjudicating body would consider the claim and owner's response. They would decide whether the claim met qualifying criteria of the 'right to reclaim abandoned property' and make a judgement on the merits of the claim and owner's response:

The adjudicating body would judge the claim against the response from the owner. They would judge:

⇨ Whether the property is more likely to be occupied if it remains under the control of the current owner or under the control of the claimants

⇨ Whether there any special circumstances which make it highly unsuitable for the property to be occupied (e.g. imminent demolition, or evidence of extreme hazard).

Outcomes of the claim

The adjudicating body can issue one of three different responses

1. If the claim meets the requirements for claim and provides the most likely prospect of the property being occupied and there are no special circumstances, the adjudicating body will issue an order providing occupation rights to the claimant.

2. If the claim does not meet the requirements for claim, does not provide a likely prospect of reuse, or if the owner's response demonstrates that the property is more likely to be reused under the owner's control the claim will be dismissed.

3. In the case of privately owned property the adjudicating body can provide a judgement, but not an order. A private owner is not bound by the judgement. The intention is that claimants address their claims with a view to reaching agreement with the owner.

Rights of owners

The owner has a right to appeal against the judgement.

The owner can also apply to regain vacant possession of the property at any time.

Both appeals are to the adjudicating body.

To be successful, an appeal to regain possession would need to demonstrate that either

⇨ The owner and the claimant have reached an agreement for the owner to regain possession.

⇨ Circumstances have changed since the original judgement to the extent that the judgement is now wrong.

⇨ The claimant has failed to bring the property into use.

⇨ The claimant is mismanaging the property.

⇨ The above information is reprinted with kind permission from Empty Homes. Please visit www.emptyhomes.com for further information.

ECO could add 10% to household fuel bills

One of the Government's supposedly green schemes to boost the energy efficiency of buildings could add 10% to the cost of household energy bills, raising fears of a consumer backlash. According to a detailed study, the Energy Company Obligation (ECO) – the sister programme to the Green Deal, is set to cost more than double the original estimate, with the additional cost set to be picked up by consumers.

The revelation came as Prime Minister David Cameron made a speech reasserting the Government's commitment to the green agenda and underlining the importance of the Green Deal and the ECO in driving energy efficiency uptake.

The ECO was introduced to pick up from previous government energy efficiency subsidy schemes, the Carbon Emissions Reduction Target (CERT) and the Community Energy Savings Programme (CESP). Under the obligation, energy companies must deliver 27.7 million tonnes of CO_2 savings by 2015. The Government has estimated that the firms will have to spend £80 per tonne of CO_2, resulting in £1.3 billion of spending each year.

But researcher Encraft's study found that the cost was more likely to be £180 per tonne of CO_2, resulting in spending of £2.9 billion each year – more than double the Government's estimate.

Spokesman Matthew Rhodes said the Department of Energy and Climate Change's (DECC) impact assessment ignored a lot of costs involved in delivering ECO.

'These hidden costs might include refitting kitchens and moving services and even DECC admit this could easily amount to £5,000 per project. Our model used much more accurate cost estimates, particularly for internal wall insulation,' he said.

Rhodes said the additional cost to energy companies would likely be levied on consumers' energy bills, with the spending increase equivalent to about a 10% uplift in the price of energy bills.

With energy bills at an all time high – and the Government pitching its energy efficiency programmes as a means to reduce them – the revelation that the ECO could drive up their cost has sparked concern among industry leaders that the scheme could be hit by a consumer backlash.

Bolstering the Government's energy efficiency programmes is a key part of Building's 'Green for Growth' campaign.

Sustainability expert David Strong warned of a 'back bench revolution against anything that would suggest a rise in consumer bills', which could undermine the Government's commitment to energy efficiency.

Shadow Energy Minister Luciana Berger said more retrofit work would need to be carried out through the ECO due to the Government's failure properly to incentivise the Green Deal.

She added that it would be 'wrong' for the public to have to pay more 'because ministers can't get their sums right'.

But a spokesperson for DECC said the Government had greater powers to monitor costs and how they were passed onto consumers under the new scheme than ever before. 'We are already seeing that ECO measures can be delivered cost effectively on the ground,' he added.

12 February 2013

⇨ The above information is reprinted with kind permission from Green Building Press. Please visit www. greenbuildingpress.co.uk for further information.

Eco-towns: the best way forward

Eco-towns should be designed so that homes will be within 400 metres of public transport 'nodes' and within 800 metres of local shops and services, according to detailed guidance published by the Town and Country Planning Association in collaboration with the Government.

Professor David Lock CBE MRTPI was recently commissioned by Communities and Local Government (CLG) to provide practical advice to help potential bidders, local authorities and others on how the eco-towns initiative can be taken forward.

This is part of the drive to create more affordable homes set in communities that are sustainable in environmental, social and economic terms.

The scoping report published this week is the first publication by TCPA and David Lock on eco-towns.

It is distinct from CLG's *Eco-towns Prospectus*, published 23 July 2007; this report provides more in-depth preliminary ideas on criteria and other independent practitioner advice on the first stage of the eco-towns programme.

Drawing on practical experience, the TCPA recently carried out, on behalf of CLG, a review of emerging good practice in urban extensions and new settlements.

This drew a number of conclusions:

⇨ the need for regional and sub-regional planning;

⇨ longer-term time horizons;

⇨ linked new settlements;

⇨ comprehensive land assembly;

⇨ the need for a specialised team;

⇨ the need for consensus; and

⇨ the importance of upfront investment.

Gideon Amos of the TCPA said: 'The primary opportunity presented by the development of an eco-town as a form of new settlement is cost efficiency in putting in place new infrastructure at the outset through initial planning. Laying down entirely new, rather than relying on old, infrastructure – whether it be physical, social or environmental – is much more cost effective than in existing urban locations.'

Applying these lessons to eco-towns, this report starts with an understanding of sustainability as a 'three legged stool' encompassing environmental, social and economic criteria.

⇨ **Environmental** Consideration must be given to energy and CO_2, water, materials, waste, transport and access, health and well-being, ecology and green infrastructure, food and urban form and land use.

⇨ **Economic** As much employment as possible should be within, or accessible from, the community. Consideration will need to be given to how the community is networked, and how employment will be supported and sustained.

⇨ **Social** Sustainable communities should be of a scale and mix to at least be able to support a secondary school (at least 4,000 to 5,000 homes) and should form clusters of places that together can support a higher order of social and economic activity.

Along with public transport nodes, also highlighted by the TCPA advice is the need for car-free areas, 15mph speed limits, generous provision of public open space and allotments and a call that new homes should be fitted with rainwater harvesting.

The association has suggested that eco-towns which want to be 'exemplars' in terms of transport should aim that no more than 25 per cent of all journeys should be by private car.

These recommendations are set out in a series of eco-town worksheets just published which cover issues surrounding transport, water cycle management and community.

A number of the principles echo best practice in new development planning in Australia, Germany, The Netherlands and Sweden.

TCPA chief executive Gideon Amos said: 'Eco-towns, because they are new settlements, present opportunities to create a different kind of town from scratch, meeting the highest standards in terms of sustainable development and minimising carbon footprints, social justice and inclusive communities.'

Other work sheets will be published shortly on green infrastructure, housing and inclusive design, waste and recycling, energy and 'green collar' jobs.

⇨ The above information is reprinted with kind permission from the Resource for Urban Design Information (RUDI). Please visit www.rudi.net for further information.

© *Resource for Urban Design Information (RUDI) 2013*

Greenhouse: where sustainability lives and works

Introduction

The award-winning Greenhouse project in Leeds is the UK's most pioneering low-carbon, mixed-use development is Citu's most ambitious project to date. From the very beginning, Citu set out to champion regeneration and set the benchmark for sustainable development.

Greenhouse is a part-refurbishment and part-new-build of a redundant art-deco hostel in South Leeds. The distinctive development comprises 166 one, two and three-bedroom apartments plus high-specification creative office space.

Winner of over 30 awards now (including the UK Green Building Council Sustainability Award), Greenhouse sets the standard for the future of sustainable development.

The concept for Greenhouse is unique yet refreshingly simple; a collection of distinctive homes and offices powered by sustainable energy, with an emphasis on strong community spirit.

The design, location, on-site amenities, leading-edge sustainable technology and residents of this building have all made this possible. Greenhouse represents a new way of life that unites and delivers all the dynamics desired for sustainable living.

A part refurbishment of a classic 1930's building, the design ethos embraces the history of the building with exposed concrete, timber and brickwork combined with contemporary statement colours, fabrics and retro-chic furniture. The combination of rooftop wind turbines, solar panels, ground source heating, and central rain and grey water tanks create sustainable energy to support everyday living and working, without compromising on design, function or quality.

The spacious courtyard provides the ideal setting for socialising with neighbours, and on-site amenities such as the gym, deli, conference space and vintage bike club, not to mention the nearby allotments, only help to strengthen the sense of community.

The award-winning Greenhouse development is ideally situated in the Beeston area of Leeds, within a 15-minute walk of Leeds Railway Station. Outside of the development, a number of shops, pubs, and eateries are opportunely positioned in the immediate vicinity. Located just off the M621, Greenhouse is well-connected to the M62 taking you East to West and the M1 taking you North to South.

The distinctive homes at Greenhouse will save the average resident around £600 a year on their energy bills. So what's good for the environment is also good for your pockets.

Greenhouse is already award winning and is often hailed as being ahead of its time, having combined cutting edge technology with industry leading sustainability measures – but we didn't build it to win awards.

We believe we should all have the choice of living a more sustainable lifestyle, and hope that with Greenhouse we've made this more achievable.

Features

Every Greenhouse home comes with a number of innovative and luxurious features as standard, including:

⇨ Heating and cooling to each apartment (via ground source heat pumps) reduces heating costs.

⇨ Monitor electricity usage and water consumption on your TV to help reduce your bills.

⇨ Dual flush W.C. with concealed cistern using recycled grey water reduces water bills.

⇨ Re-use and recycling of waste water from basins and showers uses lower cost water.

⇨ Latest thermally efficient GRP double glazing throughout, significantly reducing heating bills.

⇨ Responsibly sourced solid bamboo work tops with feature chopping board.

⇨ Touch control 'A' rated energy efficient ceramic hob, keeps electricity bills as low as possible.

⇨ A+ rated fridge (using up to 60% less energy and saving up to £13 per year).

⇨ A+ rated freezer (using up to 60% less energy and saving up to £38 per year).

⇨ Super efficient sound and heat insulation keeps bills low and reduces noise.

⇨ Grey water recycling and rain harvesting reduces water bills by 50%.

⇨ Over 90% of lights are dedicated energy efficient fittings.

⇨ Easy recycling bin with pre-sort sections makes recycling easy.

⇨ The above information is reprinted with kind permission from Greenhouse. Please visit www.greenhouseleeds.co.uk for further information.

© Citu 2013

Major threats to the Green Belt

The Green Belt is the most popular planning policy in England and the envy of the world. It helps regenerate our cities and stops them sprawling into rural areas. As a result, no one is ever too far from true, green English countryside.

Although Green Belts often contain areas of real beauty, the quality of the landscape is not relevant to the inclusion of land within a Green Belt or to its continued protection.

The Green Belt has five purposes:

⇨ to prevent urban sprawl;

⇨ to stop neighbouring towns and cities from joining-up;

⇨ to protect the countryside;

⇨ to preserve the setting and special character of historic towns, such as Bath, York and Oxford; and

⇨ to assist in urban regeneration, by encouraging the recycling of derelict and other urban land.

Once Green Belts have been defined, land within them has many positive roles to play: providing access to the countryside and nature for people in towns and cities; protecting important farmland; and mitigating against the impact of climate change by improving urban air quality and acting as a flood plain. Local food webs can also thrive within Green Belts, giving people in cities access to fresh, local produce and helping to reduce food miles.

In both the 2010 Coalition Agreement and the National Planning Policy Framework (NPPF), published in March 2012, the Government stated clearly that it attaches great importance to the Green Belt and that it will seek to maintain existing levels of protection. Yet, evidence gathered by CPRE shows that Green Belts are under threat across England.

A number of significant harmful developments in the Green Belt have recently been approved. They include:

⇨ a hotel development in connection with the expansion of Chester Zoo;

⇨ a new leisure resort in Leatherhead, Surrey;

⇨ two housing developments totalling 665 dwellings in Thurrock;

⇨ warehouses near Wakefield connected to a proposed community stadium; and

⇨ an out-of-town shopping centre in York.

Three of these cases (Chester, Leatherhead and York) were granted without a public inquiry.

All this is taking place while enough brownfield land remains available, according to the Government's own National Land Use Database, to accommodate over 1.5 million new dwellings and still more for commercial and industrial development.

Major threats to the Green Belt by region

East Midlands

⇨ Nottingham and Derby Green Belt: Secretary of State, Eric Pickles, has allowed the widening of the A453 along a 9 km stretch through the Green Belt, cutting through the largely open landscape of the Nottinghamshire Wolds. This road-widening will lead to the loss of 59 hectares (ha) of farmland, and increased levels of noise pollution. UK Coal has submitted an application for 130-ha opencast mine in Green Belt land in Broxtowe, treasured by many as 'DH Lawrence country'.

East of England

⇨ Cambridge Green Belt: plans for up to 12,350 new dwellings.

South East – London (Metropolitan) Green Belt

⇨ Bedfordshire: plans for 2,500 new dwellings at Leighton Buzzard and a 52-ha freight interchange at Sundon.

⇨ Hertfordshire: decision awaited from Eric Pickles on a massive railfreight interchange development on land at Radlett.

⇨ Surrey: planning permission granted for a hotel and golf course at Cherkley Court near Leatherhead

which would seriously affect the landscape quality of the Green Belt and the Surrey Hills Area of Outstanding Natural Beauty. Eric Pickles has decided not to call the application in for his decision.

North East – Tyne and Wear Green Belt

⇨ Durham: plans to build 3,550 new dwellings and 27 ha of business park-related development on Green Belt land around the city of Durham.

⇨ Newcastle-Gateshead: plans for 3,000 houses and a link road.

North West Green Belt

⇨ Chester and Halton: plans for 5,870 new dwellings.

⇨ Fylde: a new road at Queensway, Lytham St Annes – granted planning permission by the Secretary of State – will link to 1,150 new dwellings to be built on greenfield land outside the Green Belt. A key factor in persuading the Secretary of State was the pledge that the developer would also fund another road through the Green Belt (the M55 link) at a later date.

⇨ Heysham: Lancashire County Council has applied to the Secretary of State for permission to build a 4.8 km dual carriageway and 600-space park and ride site, most of which will involve building in the North Lancashire Green Belt.

⇨ Sefton and West Lancashire: Sefton council are likely to release Green Belt land to accommodate up to 6,600 houses. West Lancashire will propose to release 135 ha of Green Belt land to accommodate 750 houses.

⇨ St Helens: proposal for a 762-ha freight terminal on Green Belt land at Parkside.

South and West Yorkshire Green Belts

⇨ Doncaster: a new road approved by the council covers 89 ha of countryside, most of it in the Green Belt. It is intended to help bring about further new housing and business park development in the area surrounding the road.

⇨ Kirklees: plans for 1,500 dwellings on Green Belt land around Dewsbury to be examined by the Planning Inspectorate.

⇨ Leeds: consultation completed on proposals for 19,400 new dwellings on greenfield extensions to the urban area; most, if not all of the land affected, will be in the Green Belt.

⇨ Wakefield: in June 2012 the Secretary of State stated that he was 'minded to approve' an application for a community stadium and warehousing on 86 ha of Green Belt land separating Wakefield from Leeds. Despite the Secretary of State making approval conditional on the delivery of the stadium, there are widespread concerns locally that the warehousing (which would involve 50 ha of Green Belt land) will be developed without the stadium.

South West

⇨ Avon Green Belt: park and ride expansion on high quality farmland and plans for up to 4,500 new dwellings outside Bath.

West Midlands

⇨ Birmingham: proposals for 3,000 houses near Bromsgrove;

⇨ Warwick: proposals for 2,000 new houses on Green Belt land.

This brief survey of Green Belt threats is not intended to be comprehensive but includes a selection of significant cases notified by CPRE branches and members. We believe the Government should provide a full national analysis and act accordingly. For more details and case studies read our full briefing at http://bit.ly/NErJyW.

28 August 2012

⇨ The above information is reprinted with kind permission from the Campaign to Protect Rural England. Please visit www.cpre.org.uk for further information.

© Campaign to Protect Rural England 2013

Key facts

- The private rented sector has been growing in recent years and is at its highest level since the early 1990s. (page 1)

- Average weekly rents in the private sector have continued to be well above those in the social rented sector (£164 per week compared with £83). (page 1)

- For those aged between 22 and 29 across England, the average deposit is 229% of net annual salary – in London it is 300%. (page 2)

- 22-29 year olds need to save 50% of their discretionary monthly income every month for more than ten years. (page 2)

- Between 1982-1998 first-time buyers needed an average of a 5% deposit. Between 1999-2007 that number rose to 10% and since 2008 it has increased to 20%. (page 3)

- 44% of Britons believe that their children or future children won't be able to afford a decent home. (page 3)

- House prices in March 2013 were 2.7% higher than the year before. In London the figure was 7.6%. (page 4)

- In 2012, the cost of buying a home in London rose by an average of £28,000. (page 5)

- In 2012, the number of properties sold for under £200,000 fell by 7% across England and Wales. (page 5)

- One in four Londoners now rents privately. (page 11)

- Shelter reports that nearly half of London's renters have only £100 or less disposable income once essentials such as rent, fuel bills, food and council tax have been paid for. (page 11)

- 26% of ethnic minority households lived in social housing. (page 12)

- 44% of households in social housing have an annual income of less than £10,000. (page 13)

- Construction in the North West has fallen by 47% since its peak in 2007/08. (page 16)

- At the height of the economic boom, England was building 170,000 new homes a year. The annual average between 1998 and 2007 was 150,000 new homes. (page 16)

- Between 2001 and 2011, about 1.4 million new homes were built in England, while the population rose by just under four million. (page 16)

- In England there are around 280,000 homes that are empty for more than six months. (page 18)

- The Joseph Rowntree Foundation estimates that the difference between housing demand and supply will have widened into a yawning gap of 1.1 million homes in England alone by 2022. (page 19)

- More than 75,000 households were found to be homeless by local authorities in 2011/12. (page 23)

- Since 2009, the UK has spent almost £2 billion in temporary housing for homeless families – enough to build 72,000 homes. (page 26)

- 54% of the British public are concerned that removing planning permission will worsen the quality of their neighbourhood. (page 27)

- It has been calculated that 360,000 high-rise flats built between 1950 and 1980 in London alone could be torn down to make way for around 600,000 new houses and flats. (page 31)

- In Scotland, the government has invested £4.5 million in its Empty Homes Local Fund. Of this total, £2 million is being targeted at renovating empty homes in rural areas. (page 32)

- There are around 25,000 empty homes across Scotland that are classed as long-term empty; located in rural, urban and island communities. (page 33)

Bedroom Tax

A change in housing benefit to pay less money to those in a council or housing association property that is considered to have one or more spare rooms.

Discretionary Income

The money a person has remaining after taxes, mandatory charges and essential spending has been deducted.

Eco-friendly

Policies, procedures, laws, goods or services that have a minimal or reduced impact on the environment.

Help-to-buy

A scheme offered by the government that gives prospective home-buyers the opportunity to take out an interest-free loan or where the government acts as a guarantor for some of the borrower's debt.

Housing Benefit

Money provided by the government to help meet housing costs for rented accommodation for those that would be unable to do so alone.

Housing deposit

An amount of money paid to secure a property.

Greenbelt land

A policy to prevent urban sprawls into rural areas – designates land which must remain largely undeveloped.

Mortgage

A loan taken out to pay for a property which is paid back with interest.

Owner/occupier

An occupant that owns the home they live in.

Social Housing

Accommodation which is owned by the government or local authority and then rented to tenants with the aim of providing affordable housing.

Sustainable

Something that is capable of being maintained at a particular rate or level.

Assignments

1. Read *English housing survey* on page one and write an article for your local newspaper summarising the survey's findings.

2. Using the table on page two, calculate how many years it would take for a 24-year-old, earning £21,000 a year and living in the East Midlands to save for a deposit. You should assume that every month 70% of their income is assigned to taxes, mandatory charges and essential spending such as bills, rent, etc.

3. Read *Housing: are we creating a new bubble?* on page four. Summarise, in bullet points, John Humphrys' key arguments regarding the housing crisis in Britain.

4. In pairs, discuss why first time buyers are now richer and younger than they have previously been.

5. Using the information in *Chapter 1: Buying and renting*, discuss in groups whether you believe people should buy or rent.

6. Create an information booklet for first-time buyers who are trying to take their first steps on to the housing ladder. You should explain the different home ownership schemes that are backed by the Government and the steps involved.

7. Write a letter to your local MP explaining why steps are needed to protect tenants from 'rogue' or dishonest landlords.

8. With a partner, create a presentation that explains social housing and housing benefit. Think about how you will make your presentation engaging and informative.

9. Research the Government's controversial 'bedroom tax'. Write a blog post summarising the 'bedroom tax' rules and giving your thoughts and feelings on whether the scheme will be beneficial or detrimental.

10. In small groups, discuss whether lifetime social housing tenancies are an outdated policy. Make some notes and feedback to the rest of your class.

11. Read *The UK's housing crises* on pages 16 to 18. What are the author's key arguments? Summarise in bullet points or short paragraphs and then discuss with a partner.

12. Choose an illustration from this book and, with a partner, discuss what you think the artist was trying to portray, and whether you think they succeeded.

13. Choose one of the stories from *The housing crisis and me* on pages 21 and 22. Create a storyboard/comic that illustrates your chosen story.

14. Imagine that you are and your family have been forced to move into a local B&B or hotel while you wait for a Council or Housing Association property to become available. Write a blog post exploring how you feel about living in such temporary accommodation. Consider how your day-to-day living and activities would be affected by the situation.

15. Walk around your local area and note down any empty properties that you see. Could any of them be converted into housing? Perhaps they could be used for other things such as a Doctor's surgery or a school? Choose one of the buildings you saw and write a proposal to your local council, suggesting an alternative use for the empty property and explaining why this would be a good idea.

16. Do you believe people should have the right to claim abandoned property? Read the article on page 34 and in discuss with a partner or in small groups.

17. Design a poster advertising 'Greenhouse' – the sustainable project in Leeds.

18. Find out about Greenbelt land in your local area. Has any of it been built on? Report back to your class.

19. Research house prices in your local area then find a person who is older than you and has lived there for a long time and talk to them about how house prices have changed. Write a report summarising your discussion.

20. Research house prices in different countries around Europe and compare them to prices in the UK. Create a graph to demonstrate your findings.

Acknowledgements

While every care has been taken to trace and acknowledge copyright, the publisher tenders its apology for any accidental infringement or where copyright has proved untraceable.

Illustrations:

Pages 11 & 31: Don Hatcher; pages 16 & 34: Simon Kneebone; pages 3 & 21: Angelo Madrid.

Images:

All images are sourced from iStock, Morguefile or SXC, except where specifically acknowledged otherwise.

page 25 © Karen Bryan

Additional acknowledgements:

Editorial on behalf of Independence Educational Publishers by Cara Acred.

With thanks to the Independence team: Mary Chapman, Sandra Dennis, Christina Hughes, Jackie Staines and Jan Sunderland.

Cara Acred

Cambridge

September 2013